Adventures in Public Service

ADVENTURES *in*

★ *Public Service* ★

The careers of eight honored men in the United States Government

by

HOWARD SIMONS	GEORGE R. STEWART
WALLACE CARROLL	HERBERT C. YAHRAES, JR.
GOVE HAMBIDGE	OSCAR SCHISGALL
E. W. KENWORTHY	MILTON MAC KAYE

Edited by Delia and Ferdinand Kuhn

with an Introduction by Robert F. Goheen
President, Princeton University

THE VANGUARD PRESS, INC.

NEW YORK

TO THE PUBLIC SERVANTS
OF THE UNITED STATES

"*. . . I believe that in recognizing these unsung heroes in many different fields, we may very well influence some of our young men and women to think in broader terms of the kind of career they want. . . .*"

JOHN D. ROCKEFELLER 3RD
at a Public Service Awards
luncheon, December 6, 1962

Contents

Contents

Introduction

Stereotypes abound in our culture. "Over-categorization is perhaps the commonest trick of the human mind. Given a thimbleful of fact, we rush to make generalizations as large as a tub." So says Gordon Allport in *The Nature of Prejudice.*

Perhaps one of the more familiar stereotypes is that imposed by many Americans upon their public servants. All too often, when we speak of a "politician," we use the word as though it meant unprincipled opportunist, while "bureaucrat" also is a common term of opprobrium. A politician, in this loose mode of thought, is a grasping, self-concerned, usually cigar-smoking "vote getter"; the bureaucrat, a grubby individual wrapped in yards of red tape with only vision enough to see as far as the boundaries of his own department; and the idea that a sense of the public good has influence on the behavior of these people tends to be dismissed.

Of course, this nation has had her share of malefactors and incompetents in the bureaucracy, her quota of scoundrels among politicians. To deny this is to deny the facts of history. But shruggingly to accept the stereotypes not only is foolish; it also is dangerous. Foolish, because—like all stereotypes—these two are based largely on ignorance or misinformation, and hence are without constructive value. Dangerous, because such an attitude inevitably undermines the best efforts of dedicated public servants and reduces the caliber of the people on whom government can hope to draw.

The facts are that literally millions of men and women in this nation's past—and today—have worked and are working intelligently, ably, and extremely hard at jobs that keep the nation's political, social, and economic life alive and healthy and moving forward.

No society can survive without some form of government; and the bigger, more important, more world-involved that society, the more complicated and demanding the task of governing it becomes. In a nation such as our own, where a fully functioning democracy carries with it the hazard of an unwieldy bureaucracy, government is an extraordinarily complex and exacting occupation. We in the United States should count ourselves truly blessed, I believe, by the number of capable men and women who, in government, serve us from a deep sense of devotion and duty.

Neither my early life, my schooling, my wartime service, nor my work as a teacher of Classics prepared me to any great extent with a knowledge of the size and complexity of our federal government, or of those who serve us all through careers in it. Not until I undertook my present duties did I begin to sense the scope and challenge of governing a great nation in a world of explosive change. Only then, and then only gradually, did I perceive the array of talent and devotion, skill and steadfastness, vision and courage we, as Americans, enjoy in our national public services.

Of those who rise to the upper ranks of the career services, almost all who serve us there could fare better financially by accepting positions outside the government. It is axiomatic that one does not get rich in federal service. Very few will ever achieve personal renown. The average public servant may never have his name known outside a close circle of colleagues. Many will suffer the frustrations inherent in dealing with problems of crushing responsibility, of far-reaching import. But measured against these disadvantages, there exists among a great majority of those who choose careers of public service an inner sense—a warming sense—of the importance of their work in the scheme of things. There *is* excitement, there *is* challenge, there *is* progress, there *is* public responsibility.

At first glance there may seem to be little to bind together eight men whose lives are described in this book —little in common among eight very different men, and among their widely separated careers. But a thoughtful reader will find certain parallels, if not of experience, then of quality.

To be sure, the man who was for ten years our Chief Forester (Richard E. McArdle) is different from the scientist who was one of the architects for the National Aeronautics and Space Administration (Hugh L. Dryden); the man who has sought to extend security to as many of America's 180 million people as he can reach (Robert M. Ball) bears no surface resemblance to the man whose polished skills are diplomatic negotiation, intelligence analysis, and the formulation of foreign policy (Llewellyn E. Thompson). Differences certainly exist between the meticulous expert on income tax legislation (Colin F. Stam) and the man whose entire adult life has been concerned with the science of plant nutrition and growth (Sterling B. Hendricks); between the physician skilled in psychiatry and public health who devotes his energies to the prevention and treatment of mental illness (Robert H. Felix) and a geologist whose province is the "use and renewal of natural resources" (Thomas B. Nolan).

There are, however, two important similarities among all eight of these men. First, each has achieved true distinction in his life's work. Second, in each case that life's work has been in the public service. These similarities account for their appearance in this volume. But there is other and ample justification for telling of these men within the pages of a single book. Each of them represents in his life and devotion to duty the legion of able and dedicated men and women who serve us in every branch of government service.

That these eight are recognized in this book—and together—derives also from their status as winners of Rockefeller Public Service Awards. The RPS Awards were established at Princeton University in 1951 through the generosity of John D. Rockefeller, 3rd, and as a direct result of his concern for the reputation (or "image," as it would be called nowadays) of the United States Foreign Service and the United States Civil Service.

In the early 1950's the morale and prestige of the American federal civilian services were at low ebb. Vicious, headline-seeking allegations of malfeasance were concurrent with the exposure of certain internal weaknesses in government offices which caused the shadow of doubt to be cast upon the loyalty of men in responsible positions and upon the honesty of even the lowliest clerical worker. Against this setting Mr. Rockefeller, an alumnus and charter trustee of the University, came to Harold W. Dodds, then Princeton's president, and said, in effect: "I know from years of association with many people in both the Foreign Service and the Civil Service that the attacks upon them are unfair and unfounded, that the dishonesty now being highly publicized in a few cases is not representative. I know that there is great talent, great dedication, and deep integrity in the vast majority of our public servants. I wonder if together we cannot do something to correct the grossly erroneous picture now being painted in the mind of the public about its federal services."

From this concern sprang the program known as Rockefeller Public Service Awards, which are administered as a national trust by the Woodrow Wilson School of Princeton University. During the program's first seven years it was, in the main, a fellowship program that permitted certain outstanding careerists in the federal service to take sabbatical leave from their government posts for the purpose of filling gaps in their education, broadening their outlook, renewing and strengthening their knowledge in fields where great changes had taken place since the days of their formal schooling. Nominations were invited annually from all the federal agencies and these were screened by a committee of distinguished citizens outside of government. The Awards, enabling the recipients to take leaves from their posts without financial sacrifice to themselves, were made by the Trustees of Princeton University with the funds personally donated by Mr. Rockefeller to Princeton for this purpose.

In those first seven years of what we now call the "old program," Mr. Rockefeller contributed nearly a million dollars, and the program supported seventy-nine highly competent winners. An urban planner from the District of Columbia used his grant to study planning and land use in nine European capitals. An attorney from the Securities and Exchange Commission was enabled to study the regulation of investment companies in the United Kingdom. A soil chemist from the Department of Agriculture, on the verge of assuming administrative responsibilities, went to Harvard to study public administration. A geologist whose concern is the conservation of fresh water in one of our populous seacoast areas studied Dutch methods of controlling the encroachment of salt water into fresh ground-water resources.

The availability of such opportunities proved fruitful and almost at once showed the need for a much broader program, one of a scale which only the government itself could carry. The result was the Government Employees Training Act passed by the Congress and signed by President Eisenhower in 1958. His acknowledgment of the influence of RPS Awards upon the enactment of this legislation was, we felt, a superb tribute to the worth of the "old program."

With the passage of the law (Public Law 85-507) the need for privately financed mid-career study awards seemed largely to have been supplanted, and discontinuation of the Rockefeller Public Service Awards program was contemplated. So many persons, however, both in and out of the federal government, spoke of the continuing need for private efforts to foster public recognition of the scope and high quality of the work being done by dedicated public servants, that Princeton University agreed to continue directing the program, and Mr. Rockefeller has continued his support.

The "new program" retains the undergirding purpose of the original program: to enhance the prestige and improve the morale of those who devote their lives to public service. While the early series of Awards was based on the promise of the individual, the present one recognizes high distinction already achieved. Because pressing responsibilities and intensely active lives make it impossible for winners to take "sabbaticals" from their duties, Rockefeller Public Service Award winners now receive, instead, a $5,000 cash prize—tax-free and with no strings attached. They are then invited to make a further personal contribution toward strengthening the idea and ideals of public service—as, for example, by writing or lecturing, or by visits to colleges and university campuses to participate in seminars and in informal gatherings of faculty and students interested in their particular fields of endeavor. For these purposes additional funds are available to each Award winner.

That the young men and women of our nation should be able to regard the public service as a worthy and rewarding life's work is a necessity beyond question. Without a steady input into government posts of young talent of the highest levels of ability and dedication, this country could not but expect to stumble and falter in its role as world leader, and it well might fail to survive. As offsets to such dire possibilities we all owe, I feel, great gratitude to the vision and generosity of Mr. John D. Rockefeller, 3rd, and to the willing participation of the other distinguished citizens who yearly have given much good time and attention to the work of the Committee of Selection of the Rockefeller Public Service Awards. In these Awards, as in the Woodrow Wilson School as a whole, Princeton University welcomes the opportunity to strengthen and hold high the cause of career service in the various agencies of the United States government.

The eight men about whom this book is written would, to a man, deny that their stories are "inspiring." Nevertheless, these chapters do, without question, reflect a deep and abiding sense of pride and purpose and offer rich and vivid understanding of what government service can mean—to a nation, and to those who serve. In a very real sense these pages stir memories of Woodrow Wilson's call for "the deeply human man, quick to know and to do the things that the hour and his nation need."

Robert F. Goheen

President's Room
Princeton University
May 1, 1963

HUGH L. DRYDEN

Deputy administrator of "the agency responsible for getting Americans to the moon, and eventually to the planets beyond."

Photo by Jiji Press

LLEWELLYN E. THOMPSON

He "could fathom the ways of the inscrutable Communists and wait them out at the bargaining table."

STERLING B. HENDRICKS

*He "spends his working life doing such things as measuring the invisi-
ble distances between invisible atoms in an invisible molecule."*

COLIN F. STAM

"He knows more about the background of every sentence in the revenue code . . . than any other mortal."

THOMAS B. NOLAN

"His career illustrates the possibility offered in government service for the outstanding man of science."

R O B E R T   H .   F E L I X

"No one wields more influence . . . on what is being done to combat
mental illness."

ROBERT M. BALL

He believes that "social security ought to apply to all working Americans."

RICHARD E. McARDLE

His agency "enriched a nation while face-lifting its geography."

Hugh L. Dryden

FROM KITTY HAWK TO THE MOON

HOWARD SIMONS

THE TRUSTEES OF
PRINCETON UNIVERSITY

BY VIRTUE OF THE AUTHORITY VESTED IN THEM

UNDER A PROGRAM INITIATED BY JOHN D. ROCKEFELLER 3RD

TO STRENGTHEN THE CAREER

SERVICE IN THE FEDERAL GOVERNMENT

DO HEREBY GRANT A

ROCKEFELLER PUBLIC SERVICE AWARD

TO

HUGH LATIMER DRYDEN

IN RECOGNITION OF DISTINGUISHED SERVICE

TO THE GOVERNMENT OF THE UNITED STATES

AND TO THE AMERICAN PEOPLE

Robert F. Goheen
PRESIDENT

Donald B. King
CLERK

DONE IN NASSAU HALL
PRINCETON, NEW JERSEY

HUGH L. DRYDEN

On May 25, 1961, President John F. Kennedy made a plea disguised as a statement to his fellow Americans:

"I believe that this nation should commit itself to achieving the goal, before this decade is out, of landing a man on the moon and returning him safely to earth. . . ."

Although Mr. Kennedy would make subsequent bids for space cooperation, including a joint Soviet-American moon venture, at that time he was asking the Congress and the country to race Russia to the lunar surface. It was to be the most ambitious engineering effort ever undertaken.

The decision had not been an easy one for the young President. He had been in office less than six months. He had other ambitious plans to "get the country moving again." Many of these plans would have to be sacrificed or emasculated if the space goal was to be achieved. Not everyone thought the moon was a judicious choice for American space expenditures.

But ever since the Soviets launched the world's first earth satellite on October 4, 1957, the Cold War had broken the bounds of gravity and the United States was taking a licking. Its prestige had been repeatedly and significantly tarnished by Soviet space spectaculars.

In mid-1961 there seemed to be little or no choice but for the nation to shoot for the moon, where it appeared there was still a chance to best the Soviets. This was the considered opinion of more than a dozen top Presidential advisers and space experts who were asked to help Mr. Kennedy decide what could be done in space to restore luster to American prestige.

One of the key advisers helping to make this key decision was Hugh Latimer Dryden, physicist, scientific administrator, statesman, and career government servant. Few men out of government and, perhaps, no man within government, had so shaped and so influenced for so long a period the progress and direction of American efforts in aeronautics and astronautics.

"The airplane and I grew up together," Dryden once recalled. And indeed they had.

Hugh Dryden was five years old when Orville Wright stayed aloft for twelve seconds to demonstrate that man could fly in a powered, heavier-than-air machine. It was not until 1910, however, when he was twelve years old, that Dryden saw an airplane in flight. But so indelible was this experience that fifty years later he could still

recall it was an Antoinette monoplane piloted by sports-
man aviator Hubert Latham.

A decade was to pass before Dryden got to fly in a
flying machine. By this time he had already started aeronautical research that was to lead him from a $25 per week
laboratory assistantship at the National Bureau of Standards to a Presidential appointment as deputy administrator
of the agency responsible for getting Americans to the
moon, and eventually to the planets beyond.

Many times during his long career, Dryden took advantage of a public opportunity to glance back, and then,
characteristically, to peer ahead. One such occasion was
a ceremony in Washington, D.C., at which he presented
astronaut John H. Glenn's Friendship 7 space capsule to
the Smithsonian Institution. The date was February 20,
1963, a year to the day after Glenn became the first American to orbit the earth.

Inside the Smithsonian were the venerable wood and
wing, motor and metal relics of American aviation's fledg-
ling flight. Friendship 7 was joining the Wright brothers'
fragile flying machine.

"In years," Dryden said on that day, "these two machines are separated by less than the blink of an eye in
the long history of mankind. . . . Yet, within this brief
era—less than a normal man's life span—the world has
undergone revolutionary changes, solely because man
broke the chains of gravity which bound him to earth."

With the Wright brothers' machine overhead as a reminder of things past, and Friendship 7 before him as
a reminder of things future, Dryden said: "In a sense,

Colonel Glenn's flight was as faltering and feeble a step as the flight at Kill Devil Hill. Such is the march of progress, that already an aura of obsolescence hangs over Friendship 7."

Then, peering through the magnifying lenses in the center of his spectacles that tend to give him an owlish look, Dryden told his audience that man will not be content to go to the moon and no farther. As in the early days of aeronautics, the future of space can be foreseen only dimly. The riches of space are unpredictable. "We know only," Dryden said, "that we must move forward in knowledge and practical accomplishment as we strive to discover the nature of our universe."

Hugh Dryden knew Orville Wright and he knew John Glenn. These heroes represent a particular breed of American pioneer: men who pit their skill and courage against the hazardous unknown—and win. Dryden is a pioneer of a different breed.

His early research on turbulence and its effect on aircraft helped to open the door to supersonic flight, and the full potential of his research is still to be realized. He had charge of the development of the first American guided missile to be used in combat. His insight contributed to getting the United States Air Force into advanced research and development, and the government's principal aeronautical research arm into advanced aircraft development and space research. He helped to frame the National Space Act that preserved American space efforts primarily for peaceful uses and led to the creation of the National Aeronautics and Space Administration. He is credited by many with keeping the nation's space efforts balanced between manned space flight and scientific exploration. And, as chief American negotiator, Dryden reached the first agreement for space cooperation between the United States and Soviet Russia.

If Dryden grew up with the airplane, guided missiles and space flight grew up with Dryden.

Many American Drydens claim the eighteenth-century British poet and dramatist, John Dryden, as their forebear. But not Hugh Dryden, because the facts do not support such a claim. The family tree, as far as Dryden has been able to trace it, reaches to his grandparents, farmers in Worcester County, Maryland. His mother was Nova Culver Dryden. His father, Samuel Isaac, a former schoolteacher, was the operator of a general store in Maryland's Somerset County when Hugh Dryden was born on July 2, 1898.

When he was nine years old, the family moved to Baltimore, where his father had gained employment as a streetcar conductor.

Dryden was educated in the Baltimore city school system, finishing high school in 1913, just a month shy of his fifteenth birthday. He graduated first in his class, which obligingly obscured the fact that he had received a failing grade on a school theme entitled: "The Advantages of an Airship over an Airplane." Baltimore City College, the misleading name for Dryden's high school, awarded him its Peabody Prize, the first of more than two dozen national and international honors, awards, decorations, and honorary degrees.

From high school the young scientist entered Johns Hopkins University. There he came under the influence of Joseph S. Ames, the head of the university's physics department and an early advocate of basic aeronautical research. Concomitantly, in Washington, D.C., thirty-odd miles to the south of Baltimore, a skein of events was being knitted that would inextricably bind Dryden to Ames, and both to the future of American aviation.

World War I had begun. Those Americans who had clamored for greater government interest in the airplane were being rewarded. On March 3, 1915, the Advisory Committee for Aeronautics, later to become the National Advisory Committee for Aeronautics or NACA (nah kah), came into being. A. Hunter Dupree, historian of government science, has characterized the committee as "a new kind of organization for a new problem."

It was, Dupree said, "the last product of a profoundly peaceful and fertile period of [government] bureau-building and also the first war research agency of World War I."

Congress gave the agency this mandate: to supervise and direct the scientific study of the problems of flight, with a view to their practical solution. The new agency was directed by a board of a dozen—later to become fifteen—advisers who served without compensation and who were appointed by the President. Ames was named one of the first dozen advisers.

Dryden, meanwhile, pursued his bachelor's degree in physics and mathematics, finishing Hopkins' four-year undergraduate program in three and graduating with honors. The year was 1916. Dryden was not yet eighteen. A fourth year at Hopkins earned him his master's degree, for which he wrote an essay titled simply: "The Airplane."

Shortly before war's end and before he had completed

his studies for a Ph.D., Dryden left Baltimore and went to Washington. Here he took a job at the National Bureau of Standards as a laboratory assistant. His pay—$1,200 yearly. His job—to inspect munitions gauges.

The National Bureau of Standards, like the National Advisory Committee for Aeronautics, had been founded to serve industry and government. They were, as Dupree says, established to renew the government's ability "to conduct its own business in a society dominated by a complex technology that increasingly depended upon research for guidance."

Inspecting munitions gauges was not a very great challenge for a graduate physics student aspiring to basic aeronautical research. But the Bureau's new wind tunnel was. Dryden applied for and received a transfer to the tunnel. This marked the beginning of a long and fruitful association between a man and a machine which, on more than one occasion, Dryden was to compliment as aviation's "most valuable research tool."

Leonardo da Vinci knew the principle of the wind tunnel, and stated it simply: "What an object does against the motionless air, the same does the air moving against the object at rest." The first wind tunnel on record was built by Francis H. Wenham for the Aeronautical Society of Great Britain in the 1870's. Before Wenham's tunnel, and for a time after, any number of investigators attempted any number of observational methods for determining the effect of air upon a body in flight. Shapes and surfaces and models were exposed to the breeze, dropped from the Eiffel Tower, or mounted on fast-moving vehicles. But natural wind, as Dryden has explained, is notoriously fickle, and a large volume of still air is inordinately difficult to come by. So artificial wind in a tunnel became the answer, even for the Wright brothers.

The Wrights did not put together a bicycle-shop contraption and call it a flying machine. On the contrary, the first flight at Kitty Hawk was "the culmination of a carefully planned scientific study of the problems of flight," including research with kites and gliders and wind tunnel experiments on some 200 airfoils. The Wright wind tunnel was a wooden, coffin-like affair employing a fan to achieve a 27-mile-per-hour wind. "Thus," Dryden noted on the golden anniversary of the Wright brothers' flight, "the first successful plane sprang like a genie from a little box with a feeble fan at one end."

By the time Dryden caught up with the wind tunnel it was already in wide use in Europe, although it was still relatively new in the United States. The National Advisory Committee's first wind tunnel, for example, had not yet been completed. The Bureau of Standards tunnel, therefore, was one of the earliest in government service, largely the accomplishment of the late Lyman J. Briggs, a distinguished scientist who paced his friend Dryden in promotions at the Bureau, and who eventually became its director.

If the Bureau's wind tunnel enabled Dryden to embark on his cherished course of aeronautical research, it also permitted him, with the help of Ames, to complete his Ph.D. without returning to Baltimore. The trick was for Dryden to hear Ames lecture during the professor's frequent trips to Washington, and to use the Bureau's wind tunnel at night for his university research project, which was to verify model laws. In 1919 Dryden was granted his Ph.D. He was twenty years old.

For America, as for Dryden, the "roaring twenties" were about to begin. It was to be an exciting decade, especially in aviation. In the first year NACA set the pace by proposing a national aviation policy that included: the establishment of a bureau of aeronautics in the Commerce Department; the authorization of airplane competition to stimulate new designs; and expansions of the air-mail service, government research, and air appropriations for the Army and Navy.

There were new planes and new engines and new records and new wind tunnels. And names such as Lieutenant J. H. Doolittle, Major Carl Spaatz, and Admiral Richard E. Byrd. Billy Mitchell battled for military air power, and regular commercial air service began between New York and Boston.

In 1924 the Soviets established a Central Committee for the Study of Rocket Propulsion. On March 23, 1926, America's Robert H. Goddard launched the world's first liquid-fueled rocket at Auburn, Massachusetts, sending it 184 feet in two and one-half seconds. A year later, Charles Lindbergh flew the Atlantic. And the decade ended with the German public becoming excited about interplanetary travel, all because of a movie called *The Girl in the Moon.*

It was to be an exciting decade for Dryden, too. There was a swift promotion and marriage and wind tunnel research and children and more wind tunnel research.

In 1920 he married Mary Libbie Travers, who bore him Hugh, Jr., Ruth, and Nancy. Also in 1920, at twenty-two, he was named chief of the Bureau's aerodynamical physics section. This meant that he was in charge of all wind tunnel activities at the Bureau. He began research on the problems of wind tunnel turbulence and boundary-layer flow.

One man's research is often another's inspiration. Dryden extended studies started by Germany's Ludwig Prandtl, who in turn had been inspired by England's Osborne Reynolds. Decades later, Swiss-born Werner Pfenninger would design an airplane embodying the work of all three. The critical factor in the research of these men was turbulence, first discovered by Reynolds in 1883 by studying the flow of water through pipes.

"A precise definition of turbulent flow," Dryden explained, "is somewhat technical, but as in the case of many concepts hard to define in words, every layman is familiar with the phenomena described. He has surely observed the smoke from a cigarette in a quiet room rising smoothly in layers, the motion described as laminar. At some distance above the cigarette, however, unless the air in the room is extraordinarily quiet, this smooth motion breaks up into a confused series of whirls and eddies, a motion described as turbulent."

Essentially, what happens to cigarette smoke happens to the thin layer of air next to a surface that is moving in a fluid. As first postulated by Prandtl in the early 1900's, this thin layer of air, which he called the boundary layer, changes from a smooth or laminar flow to a turbulent flow.

As a result of extensive wind tunnel experiments, Dryden and his colleagues demonstrated that plain old airflow turbulence was responsible for distorting wind tunnel measurements, and that boundary-layer turbulence, as it passes over an aircraft in flight, significantly reduces the plane's speed and range. Consequently, Dryden and his colleagues developed methods for increasing and decreasing turbulence in wind tunnels; for designing and building tunnels of low turbulence; and for obtaining the first experimental evidence to verify Prandtl's hypothesis. Dryden's basic work led to the design of improved aircraft.

A more recent continuation of Dryden's early research is the Northrop Corporation's laminar-flow-control airplane designed by Pfenninger for the United States Air Force. The X-21A, as it is called, employs air-breathing wings that inhale the boundary-layer air and expel it to the rear, reducing drag from boundary-layer turbulence by 80 per cent and increasing the range or payload-carrying capacity of a large airplane by 50 per cent, with no increase in fuel consumption. Northrop has predicted that eventually a laminar-flow-control airplane equipped with a new type of engine will be able to stay aloft for three to four days without refueling.

There were other significant research projects during the 1920's. Dryden and Army Major E. J. Loring were instrumental in redesigning and standardizing American aerial bombs that were used until the end of World War II. Together, Briggs and Dryden made the first measurements of what happens to airplane parts at and slightly above the speed of sound.

By the 1930's, aeronautical research and aviation were on firm ground. Research brought controllable-pitch propellers, retractable landing gears, automatic radio-navigation systems, and more efficient wing sections and flaps. The dirigible experienced its greatest popularity and its collapse. The decade ushered in light private planes, Pan American Clippers, and the modern airliner; the ramjet, the pure jet, and the helicopter. The people linked with these bore many of the old names and many new ones: Amelia Earhart, the Piccards, Wiley Post, Igor Sikorsky, and Alexander de Seversky.

In 1930 Germany launched its first liquid rocket as part of its nascent military program, a program that attracted Wernher von Braun two years later. In 1933 Soviet Russia successfully fired its first liquid rocket.

By decade's end, work had been almost completed on many of the fighters and bombers that would soon attack and defend freedom: Messerschmitt, Hurricane, Spitfire, P-38, P-40, Helldiver, B-24, B-25, and B-29.

During this period, Dryden's wind tunnel studies earned him an international scientific reputation. Indicative of this was an invitation in 1934 to address the International Congress of Applied Mechanics at Cambridge, England, to discuss his boundary-layer research. This was his first trip to Europe, to which he was to return time and again as a scientist exchanging scientific views, as a scientist seeking wartime secrets, and finally as a scientist seeking peacetime cooperation. This same year, 1934, also brought his promotion to be chief of the National Bureau of Standards' mechanics and sound division.

Though Dryden continued to devote the bulk of his time and thought to turbulence and boundary-layer control during the 1930's, there were diversions. There were determinations of the absolute value of gravity, and other investigations, with his associates, into the effects of wind on roofs and chimneys, on the Empire State Building, and on trains and automobiles.

Dryden and his co-workers were convinced by their wind tunnel studies that streamlined cars could go faster and use less gasoline than could the boxlike automobiles then fashionable and popular. "The reason for the delay in introducing truly streamlined cars," Dryden told a philosophical society in 1935, "lies in the repugnance of the public to radical changes in appearance. Attempts are being made by manufacturers to make a gradual transition."

Years later Dryden came back to the general subject of streamlining. Surely, he told an audience at the University of California in 1948, the most important influence of streamlining has been on the intellectual and spiritual lives of men. And by this, Dryden explained, he did not mean the application of the adjective "streamline" to furnaces, washing machines, men's shirts, and the female figure, but "to the more solid and meaningful concept of that harmony with the physical laws of the universe which enables us to live with a minimum of useless effort and disturbance.

"The streamlining of office procedures, of the committees of Congress, of specifications for materials, of college curricula—all such concepts grew out of this impact of the aeronautical development of an aircraft which traveled through the air with a minimum of disturbance, with each part functional and operating at peak efficiency. I have heard also in government bureaus of streamlining the buck so that it may more readily be passed from one office to another. But surely more important than all of these is the streamlining of one's life so that we may proceed with a minimum of friction with our neighbors, with our energies applied to the task of reaching our goals swiftly."

Calling attention to the intellectual and spiritual values in life was not a casual reference by Dryden. Throughout most of his adult life, he had been a lay preacher and a Bible teacher at the Calvary Methodist Church in Washington. For Dryden, there never was a conflict between science and religion. In his view, science, by its very nature, restricts itself to certain aspects of natural phenomena, and is, therefore, but a partial view of life. Religion, on the other hand, Dryden felt, must accept the results of scientific examination and use these results in its own interpretation of life.

In his own life, Dryden tried to maintain a balance among what he conceived to be a trinity of ethos affecting all men:

"I believe that every human life has a threefold aspect: materialistic, intellectual, and spiritual, relating to body, mind, and soul. A harmonious development of all three is required for all men, including scientists. We all have a physical body, common to the animals. If the materialistic aspects are emphasized, and the mental and moral aspects undeveloped, we find a man living like an animal: primitive, sensual. If the intellectual aspects dominate and are regarded as supreme and all-sufficient, we have the egotistical, selfish, soulless egghead who makes reason a god. If the intellectual development is neglected and the emotional aspects are supreme, we find the life dominated by instinct and emotion."

Hugh Dryden has been neither primitive nor selfish nor

dominated by emotion, whether in control of men or a ticklish scientific investigation.

Not all Dryden's aeronautical problems during the 1930's involved large vehicles. Baseballs became a challenge. Late in the decade a rhubarb flared between the American and the National leagues. Each contended the other was using a livelier baseball. At least this seemed a plausible explanation for why so many home runs were being hit and why batting averages were zooming. Dryden and his colleagues were asked to come to the aid of their countrymen's favorite pastime. After elaborate study of the problem—including field tests at ball parks—the Bureau of Standards team concluded officially that there was no appreciable difference between the standard balls being used by either league. Unofficially, they found, the difference seemed to be with Jimmy Foxx, Joe DiMaggio, Hank Greenberg, Mel Ott, and other unscientific factors.

The nation's baseball problems were soon pushed into the background. In 1940 President Roosevelt called for the production of 50,000 planes yearly, while Robert Goddard's efforts to interest the government in his rocket research failed miserably. In 1941 the Japanese attacked Pearl Harbor. Thereafter, research was gradually begun on atomic bombs and guided missiles, the swept-wing concept and afterburners, rockets and intercontinental ballistic missiles.

In June, 1944, the Germans fired the first V-1 buzz bomb. Three months later the first V-2 fell on London. A year later Hiroshima and Nagasaki were obliterated by atomic bombs. The world has not since known true peace.

No sooner had the war ended than scientists began to use rockets for studies of the upper air. In 1947 the sound barrier was broken. The year Orville Wright died (1948), three million Berliners were kept alive by a continuous relay of the machine he invented.

World War II changed the pattern of life, if not the psyche, of the nation. Dryden's life was no exception. Early in the 1940's Dryden was tapped by Vannevar Bush to serve as a consultant to the National Defense Research Committee, which Bush headed. Bush had been director of NACA. In his new position, he was to become the czar of the nation's wartime scientific effort. Dryden was told, in effect: "Look, we have a project for an automatic guided glide bomb. A small aircraft company is working on it. We'd like you to take a look at what the company is doing." Dryden not only looked into the project, but spent almost the rest of the war as director of a Navy program that developed the first American guided missile to be used in combat.

The concept was straightforward: A bomb equipped with wings to glide it and a homing device to guide it would be sent against the enemy. As with most straightforward concepts, the path to the product was tortuous and the bomb took almost three years to develop. The first glide bomb considered by Dryden's group would have employed a small television for steering the weapon to its target. But a later version—the one actually used in combat —employed a small radar that bounced signals off a target, caught them, caused the bomb to adjust its flight path by automatically maneuvering its flaps, and then plunged the bomb onto the target. This glide bomb, aptly dubbed the Bat, was used effectively against Japanese shipping during the battle of Okinawa.

Near war's end, Dryden was tapped again for a new role —this time by General H. H. Arnold, chief of the Army Air Forces. With victory in sight, Arnold foresaw the need for postwar research and development to strengthen defense through air power. To this end he established the AAF Scientific Advisory Group. The late Theodore von Karman was named director, Dryden his deputy. The group's task: to prepare a report for guiding future Air Forces research and development.

The group's first aim was to ascertain how other nations, principally the Axis powers, had adapted science to war; and so Von Karman and Dryden were in Germany on V-E Day, dressed in Army uniforms and holding the simulated ranks of general and colonel, respectively. Their first stop was Volkenrode, a laboratory near Braunschweig in north central Germany that was so cleverly hidden beneath landscaped roofs that it escaped detection until overrun by Allied troops.

Von Karman and Dryden arrived at Volkenrode just as a British team, on a similar mission, came upon the scene. What the Anglo-American searchers found were the plans, models, reports, and designs for a host of new and radical jet aircraft and missiles.

Volkenrode's director was H. Blenk, whom both American scientists had known. As a result, one interview with Blenk was worth a thousand reports. And the same situation applied throughout Germany. Von Karman and Dryden interviewed other friends and enemies, including Ludwig Prandtl, whose work at the turn of the century had set Dryden upon his own research path.

The two Americans continued through Europe, interviewing scientists and visiting other laboratories and wind tunnel installations. Finally, after a stop in England to match notes with Sir Henry Tizard, chief British defense research scientist and Bush's counterpart, the team went home.

Once back in Washington, the Air Forces group began their larger task: to evaluate their data and to look ahead. Dryden's specific assignment was to review German wartime efforts in guided-missile research and development.

The group's first overall report, "Where We Stand," was a broad evaluation of the state of missiles and rockets, supersonic aircraft, and related advances. This was followed by the twenty-volume, definitive study called *Toward New Horizons,* a survey of what the future held for aeronautics and astronautics. *Toward New Horizons* became a touchstone for Air Forces research and development activities in the late 1940's. Though the massive report anticipated many future airplane and missile programs, it did not contemplate spaceships for putting men on the moon.

Dryden said World War II had freed him from his narrow horizon of a tight little laboratory. He had been exposed to the management of a large development project and he had influenced public policy. When he left the Bureau at the war's beginning, he was still a practicing researcher. When he returned at war's end in January, 1946, it was as an assistant director. To all intents and purposes his creative laboratory days were over. Now he became a science manager.

Six months after his return to the Bureau he was promoted to associate director. When his friend and colleague Briggs retired, it was generally assumed that Dryden would be made director. But the job went to Edward U. Condon. In September, 1947, Dryden transferred to the National Advisory Committee on Aeronautics as director of aeronautical research.

Shortly before the end of the decade, George W. Lewis, director of NACA since 1915, stepped down and Dryden became director. This was a critical time for the agency. It had gone into the war with a handful of personnel and a single laboratory at Langley, Virginia. Now it had three laboratories; it was adding new people; and its annual budget was $25 million and growing.

A former colleague says: "Dryden's secret was to practice a kind of magic that caused very nearly all of the NACA people to do their very best. He was, you might say, a leader who was nearly invisible in those days, who led wonderfully well without appearing to lead."

The early 1950's brought intensified efforts to develop military and civil supersonic aircraft, and missiles of all varieties. Military piston aircraft were rapidly being replaced with jets, such as the Migs and Sabres that battled over Korea. Balloons and rockets were continuing to provide scientists with new tools for unraveling the mysteries of the solar system.

For Dryden and his agency these were busy years, marked

by significant achievements. Richard T. Whitcomb verified the so-called "area rule," which resulted in the "wasp waist" shape that added speed to jet airplanes. H. Julian Allen conceived the "blunt nose" principle that was applied to intercontinental ballistic missiles and much later, to the Mercury space capsule. A. J. Eggers and C. A. Syverton conceived the principle of "interference lift," which promised to become the most effective way of designing supersonic bombers. Research was pursued on helicopters, vertical- and short-take-off aircraft, jet engines and ramjet power plants, nuclear propulsion, and the ways in which electronic devices could aid man in flight.

The 1950's also brought countless attempts by industry to buy Dryden from government service. A former associate recalls the day a corporation asked Dryden for the third time to head a new missile division. The newest offer included a salary of more than $100,000 plus stock options. "Again Dryden declined, diffidently, almost apologetically," the associate remembers. " 'I wish they'd quit,' he told me."

Until the Korean War, NACA's research activity had been focused mainly upon problems peculiar to the airplane. But by the mid-1950's Dryden had succeeded in guiding NACA away from being just a handmaiden to aviation and toward technology aimed at space flight. Serious popular interest in space was sparked on July 29, 1955, when the White House dramatically announced that the United States planned, as its participation in the International Geophysical Year, to launch history's first artificial earth-encircling satellite. The target date was set for sometime during 1957 or 1958. The ambitious project, dubbed Vanguard, was given to the Navy to manage.

There were few doubts in 1955 that the United States, the world's undisputed master of science and technology, would achieve its stated goal. But October 4, 1957, proved differently. Soviet Russia launched Sputnik I, history's first artificial earth-encircling satellite.

Sputnik's impact was stunning. Presidential candidate John F. Kennedy would call it the "greatest blow" to American prestige since World War II. To the sophisticated and the unsophisticated alike, Sputnik came to symbolize the transformation of primarily agricultural Russia into an industrial giant capable of challenging the United States claim to scientific and technological superiority. Many Americans became self-flagellants, given over to agonizing reappraisals of their values, their school systems, their support of science and technology, and their damaged prestige.

On November 3, 1957, the Soviets launched a second Sputnik, this one carrying a dog named Laika. Attempts to get the U. S. Vanguard off the ground failed. American self-scourging continued. Finally, on January 31, 1958, the Army successfully launched Explorer I. The United States was in space. But satisfaction was not guaranteed. The national anxiety persisted.

It was clear that the national mood required two compensatory steps: a new agency to manage American space efforts, and plans to put man into space.

Dryden and NACA chairman James H. Doolittle joined members of the Bureau of the Budget and President Eisenhower's science adviser, James R. Killian, in drafting legislation for the new agency. On April 2, 1958, President Eisenhower sent a special message to Congress recommending the establishment of a National Aeronautics and Space Agency. Dryden became a key administration spokesman for the legislation.

"In essence," Dryden told the Select Committee on Astronautics and Space Exploration of the House of Representatives, "the President's recommendation is for the establishment of a new, independent federal agency that will be responsible for programs concerned with problems of space technology, space science, and civil space exploration. It is further proposed that the new agency, which I will refer to as the NASA, will use the present National Advisory Committee for Aeronautics, NACA, as its nucleus."

Though Dryden had become an astute and agile politician during his many years of government service that had necessitated his defending his agencies and programs against budget cutters and other agencies and programs, rarely had he experienced a petulant congressman. NACA had been, in Dryden's words, "completely insulated from politics," partly because it was shielded by its distinguished committee of advisers and partly because most congressmen were uninterested. After all, the agency researched vehicles; it did not build or buy them. If it was a pork barrel, it was a very shallow one. But in early 1958 congressmen became interested in NACA and in Dryden, and especially in whether the newly proposed NASA should be controlled by civilians or the military or both.

"Instead of seeking in these beginning minutes of the space age to determine in great detail the full range of future military uses of space vehicles," Dryden told the congressmen, "we might better concentrate our efforts on the many massive problems that require solution for us to explore our solar system."

It was generally assumed that Dryden would be named to head the new space agency. But his views, bluntly expressed at times, and a misunderstanding over his attitude toward manned space flight apparently combined to bring Dryden afoul of some members of Congress.

In the first flush of the space age, Wernher von Braun and others had proposed a simple spectacular that, in effect, called for tossing a man vertically upward and then recovering him by the use of a parachute. Dryden had said it would be like shooting a young lady from a cannon. His comment was widely interpreted as representing general opposition to putting a man into space because he regarded it as a circus stunt. Dryden was questioned sharply about the incident and his attitude. His explanation: This simple experiment, standing alone as an objective, is not of very much greater value than the shooting of a lady from a cannon. It gives a small amount of scientific information at a great amount of cost.

What Dryden advocated, instead, was in time to become Project Mercury. But some of the congressmen apparently were still not satisfied. In their view Dryden was too conservative for what they had in mind. This was reflected in the comment of the Select Committee chairman following Dryden's defense of his position:

"Some people thought, assuming an agency were established and you were appointed the director, the head of it, that it [the circus analogy] might indicate the state of your mind on your part where you are more wedded to past activities of your organization [NACA] than the future activities."

Dryden was not picked for the job. The National Aeronautics and Space Act of 1958 was passed by Congress on July 29 and signed by President Eisenhower on the same day. Ten days later the President nominated T. Keith Glennan, president of the Case Institute of Technology, to be the new agency's administrator, and Dryden to be deputy administrator. By October NASA declared itself ready to function, and events moved swiftly thereafter. The President promptly directed that all remaining International Geophysical Year projects being managed by the Pentagon be transferred to NASA. NASA formally organized Project Mercury to place a man in orbit around the earth, and invited industrial representatives to a briefing on a proposed one-and-one-half-million-pound-thrust engine designated F-1. By year's end NASA was in business and the IGY was ending.

The last of the decade brought intensified space efforts by the U.S. and Soviet Russia. Dryden was appointed one of two men to assist Ambassador Henry Cabot Lodge at the first meeting of the United Nations Committee on the Peaceful Uses of Outer Space. In December, 1959, largely through Dryden's activities in the preceding months, NASA proposed joint research with other nations to promote international space cooperation.

During that year, the United States launched eleven space vehicles to Soviet Russia's three moon probes. This was to become a pattern of the early competition between the two space powers. Soviet Russia, capitalizing on superior rocket power, would launch a few massive spacecraft yearly to score what the newspapers labeled "space spectaculars." The United States, with limited rocket power, would send greater numbers of smaller and more sophisticated vehicles aloft.

The United States had made the decision to build smaller rocket boosters because it had been able to reduce the size of nuclear warheads and could perfect intercontinental ballistic missiles more cheaply than could the Soviets. That was before either nation realized that the exploration of outer space would be a major ideological weapon. When the Soviets did realize that their bulkier military missiles would also serve to place enormous packages into space, they lost no time in exploiting their unwittingly begotten advantage. For the United States to gain the same advantage would mean years of effort to develop large rocket engines.

During these early NASA years, Dryden's energy, time, and talent were devoted mainly to keeping a close watch on the new agency's varied and fast-spreading scientific and technical activities. His reputation was generally credited with attracting outstanding professional talent to NASA. Indicative of his stature in the scientific community was the fact that he served as home secretary of the nongovernmental National Academy of Sciences, the nation's most august body in this field.

Dryden's leadership insured that as long as he had a say in the decision-making process, the strictly scientific aims of the nation's space program would be protected. Once skeptical himself of what could and should be done in space, he was now imploring hesitant scientists to back the nation's space aims, including exploration and manned space flight. He considered both efforts vital if the United States was to avoid "the hazard of future technological obsolescence, the hazard of potential loss of leadership, the hazard of military surprise by potential enemies."

Together with Glennan, Dryden spent hours defending and explaining these aims to policy planners, budget cutters, technical groups, decision makers, and above all, to anxious congressmen.

Soon after Mr. Kennedy took office, Glennan stepped down. But Dryden, an Eisenhower appointee and a Democrat, was asked to stay on. NASA's new administrator was James E. Webb, a successful businessman, a former Under Secretary of State, and a former Director of the Budget Bureau.

Dryden's role at NASA began to change. Robert C. Seamans, Jr., had been appointed associate administrator and general manager. Together, Webb, Dryden, and Seamans became a "troika" for managing NASA. Seamans was given charge of the day-to-day operations. This essentially freed Dryden to concentrate on major policy matters.

The team of Webb and Dryden made an incongruous but complementary pair. This was apparent whenever the two appeared in tandem before congressional committees or reporters. Webb, mellifluous, aggressive, gregarious, politically acute and politically sensitive, spoke faster than the speed of sound and looked much like a middle-aged cherub. Dryden was thought-careful and word-cautious, wryly humorous, quick to smile a tight smile and almost always soft-spoken, dressed in somber suits with vest to match, possessing facial features that seemed to have come from a Grant Wood canvas.

Together, Webb, Dryden, and Seamans brought NASA into the 1960's, and the 1960's, in turn, brought men to space—Shepard, Grissom, Glenn, Carpenter, Schirra, Cooper, as well as Gagarin, Titov, Popovich, and Nikolayev. There would be weather and communications and navigation satellites; orbiting observatories to measure the earth and to observe the sun and the moon, the planets and the stars; plans for manned space stations; and nuclear rockets and boosters as tall as the Statue of Liberty. There would be spacecraft to fly around or past or to land on the moon and Mars and Venus—two-man craft and three-man craft.

And so, in May, 1961, President Kennedy put the United States in the space race. The whole job of getting a man to the moon and back would cost every man, woman, and child in the nation at least $100. NASA would spend in one week Dryden's total annual budget for NACA during 1958, its last year. NASA would come to affect the nation's economy, education, research, and politics—its self-image and its image abroad.

"The NASA was created," Dryden said a year after the President's moon message, "to carry out a program that would explore space in the best interests of the United States and of men everywhere. To open space to gain additional knowledge of the universe in which man lives, to open space as a demonstration of this country's mastery of advanced technology, to share what we discover with humanity as a whole—these reflect a concept of world leadership which, I am convinced, reasonable men in all nations approve."

Dryden meant "all nations," for a month earlier he had held the first of a year-long series of talks with Soviet academician Anatoli A. Blagonravov on the possibility of space cooperation between the United States and Soviet Russia. The talks grew out of correspondence between Premier Nikita S. Khrushchev and President Kennedy, who had appointed Dryden the nation's chief negotiator. In March, 1963, Dryden and Blagonravov signed an agreement in Rome that essentially called for cooperation in a communications-satellite experiment, the coordinated launching of weather satellites, and scientific satellites to map the earth's magnetic field. The agreement was heralded as a first step toward more effective space cooperation between the two nations in the future.

It was obvious, however, that the space competition between the United States and Soviet Russia would continue. Twice in the 1900's the United States scrambled from behind to overtake competitors and recapture the lead. The Wright brothers made their historic flight in 1903, but when World War I began the United States had only 24 military airplanes compared to France's 1,400, Germany's 1,000, Russia's 800, and England's 400. Goddard sent the world's first liquid rocket aloft in 1926, but when World War II began he and his work were ignored by the government. For aviation and for space flight, it seemed that the American frontier was earth-bound.

When the nation did decide to catch up, however, it moved with speed and prowess. I believe that this, plus the dedication of men such as Hugh Dryden, guarantees the nation's eventual success. With an agreed plan to reach the moon and beyond, American officials were confident that it would be only a matter of time before the Soviets were bested in space.

Of the future, Dryden had this to say:

"None of us knows what the final destiny of man may be, or if there is any end to his capacity for growth and adaptation. Wherever this venture leads us, I am convinced that the power to leave the earth—to travel where we will in space and to return at will—marks the opening of a brilliant new stage in man's evolution."

Of Dryden, Glennan had this to say:

"His central belief that the dignity of man stems from his creation in the image of God must certainly have carried him over some very rough spots in the in-fighting which characterizes a fair portion of the Washington scene. His willingness always to go the second mile, unless a matter of important principle is involved, has bridged the shoals of controversy in innumerable cases. Never a man to promise more than he thought he could deliver, his vision has been more sound than that of most of his contemporaries and in no way less far-reaching. A lifetime in government service has taught him something of the value of patience, and his own integrity has steered him away from unwise compromises."

Llewellyn E. Thompson

THE DIPLOMAT AND THE ENIGMA

WALLACE CARROLL

THE TRUSTEES OF
PRINCETON UNIVERSITY

BY VIRTUE OF THE AUTHORITY VESTED IN THEM

UNDER A PROGRAM INITIATED BY JOHN D. ROCKEFELLER 3RD

TO STRENGTHEN THE CAREER

SERVICE IN THE FEDERAL GOVERNMENT

DO HEREBY GRANT A

ROCKEFELLER PUBLIC SERVICE AWARD

TO

LLEWELLYN E. THOMPSON

IN RECOGNITION OF DISTINGUISHED SERVICE

TO THE GOVERNMENT OF THE UNITED STATES

AND TO THE AMERICAN PEOPLE

PRESIDENT

CLERK

DONE IN NASSAU HALL
PRINCETON, NEW JERSEY

LLEWELLYN E. THOMPSON

"Russia," said Winston Churchill with the rumpled perplexity of a man who has been hugged by a bear, "Russia is a riddle wrapped in a mystery inside an enigma."

The man who represents the United States in this forbidding country must live with the riddle while he seeks to penetrate the mystery and explain the enigma to his uneasy principals at home.

No doubt this was already true enough in 1781 when Francis Dana and his young secretary, John Quincy Adams, arrived at the court of Catherine the Great to seek recognition for the rebellious American colonies.

It is all the more true today when the United States and the Soviet Union confront each other, with the power of mutual annihilation.

To this exposed and sensitive post in the summer of 1957 came a new American ambassador. After nearly thirty years on the diplomatic circuit in Asia, Europe, and America, Llewellyn Thompson was not entirely a riddle or an enigma to the Soviet officials and the members of the diplomatic corps who welcomed him at the Moscow airport.

In fact, he was known in the trade as a political analyst of exceptional quality, an accurate reporter, and a tireless and resourceful negotiator. In his custody a secret of state was as secure as in Fort Knox. But in the drawing room he had a flow of small talk and patter that he could easily adjust to suit his audience—male or female, undergraduate or septuagenarian, Anglo-Saxon, Latin, or Byzantine. Indeed, Gilbert and Sullivan might have touted him as the very model of a Foreign Service officer.

One thing, however, his fellow diplomats might have overlooked that July day at the airport. Thompson had achieved all this—and a wardrobe out of Savile Row—without ever forfeiting his Colorado birthright. His long lean face, ruddy skin, and clear blue eyes would have looked at home above a cow pony. And for all his long years abroad he had kept certain American qualities—shrewdness and good sense rather than intellectualism, a bent for humor rather than wit, and whatever it is that addicts a man to the peculiarly American game of poker.

The Foreign Service of the United States has never been confused in the popular mind with the Marine Corps. On Capitol Hill in Washington the kindly men who vote its budget sometimes refer to its members as "the striped-pants boys" or "the cookie-pushers."

Thompson was a member of—indeed a product of—this brotherhood. It is possible that at one time or another an outsider had sized him up as one of the striped-pants boys. Yet in five years in Moscow he was to play a cool hand, to uphold the American point of view in argument with the most dangerous man to come on the world scene since the last great war, and to become within a few weeks of his return home the President's most trusted adviser on matters of war or peace with the mysterious Russians.

Who was he, then? Where did he come from? How did he learn his job? And how did he rise to the top of his profession?

Llewellyn E. Thompson, Jr., was born at Las Animas, Colorado, on August 24, 1904. His father was a rancher—a sheep- and cattleman. This was a feast-and-famine business at best, and in Thompson's boyhood it seems to have been mostly famine. At the age of twelve he started working at odd jobs to raise spending money, and he continued working through high school—as janitor in an office building, clerk in a hardware store, and ticket agent for the Sante Fe railroad.

Times still were hard when he entered the University of Colorado in 1923. That first year he washed dishes to help pay his way. The next, he became manager of the Delta Tau Delta house and earned his room and board. In the summer, with a friend, he turned the establishment into a boarding house for girls and filled it with the daughters of rich Texans fleeing the heat of the plains.

"That's where I first learned about diplomacy," he says.

For a year he was out of school, working as an accountant for the Mid-West Refining Company in Wyoming. Then he returned to Colorado. His major was in economics.

It was the Jazz Age—the time of Valentino haircuts,

John Held trousers, and campus wits who thrived all semester on "Oh yeah?" It was also the time of prohibition, and students at Colorado, like students at other institutions of higher learning, were doing significant things with corn mash and copper tubing, or malt and hops and yeast.

One of these noble experiments almost derailed Thompson. The authorities raided the quarters he shared with three other students and found not only a mess of beer that the four had concocted but also a gallon of grain alcohol stored there by an old grad against the pains of a class reunion.

Thompson escaped expulsion, but as punishment he was compelled to drop one course. This was just enough to keep him from graduating that year. Eventually he made up the course by mail and received his A.B. from Colorado in the same way. That was in 1928.

"The first time I ever went to a college commencement," he says, "was when I got an honorary degree from Harvard in 1961."

Before he left school Thompson had thought of going into the importing business. He made a trip to Seattle and talked to a number of importers. They told him that importing was generally carried on by small companies with limited staffs, and they suggested that he try for some experience abroad by joining the Foreign Service.

On a steamer going from Seattle to Los Angeles, Thompson met a retired Foreign Service officer. This man, a former consul, encouraged him to apply for the Foreign Service, and Thompson decided that this was what he wanted to do.

In the year after graduation he moved to Washington and took a cram course for the Foreign Service examination. The Foreign Service in those days was a tight little club with membership confined largely to men with an Ivy League patina. A candidate from a Western cow college had the odds against him.

Thompson did well in his written examination but gave what he still believes was a dismal performance in the orals.

"The truth is," he says, "I barely got in."

His first appointment was as vice-consul at Colombo in Ceylon. For four years he did the routine of a consulate in a big Asian port—visas and passports, the paper work of commerce, all the problems created by American seamen in trouble and American travelers out of funds in a strange country.

Then, in 1933, he was transferred, still a vice-consul, to the consulate in Geneva.

How great an opportunity the new post offered, Thompson could not have realized at first. Geneva was a world capital, the seat of the League of Nations. Prime ministers, foreign ministers, the outstanding ambassadors met there to transact business. All the big unmanageable problems sooner or later came before the League—disarmament, Mussolini's invasion of Ethiopia, Hitler's occupation of the demilitarized zone in the Rhineland, the Spanish civil war, the Japanese invasion of North China. And the American consulate in Geneva was a great deal more than a consulate. It was a listening post at the League, a chancery that gathered political and economic intelligence and kept

Washington informed of all the Geneva maneuvers.

Thompson was all the more lucky because his mentor in Geneva was the late Prentiss Gilbert, the American consul. On Gilbert's staff at the time were at least three other young officers who were to rise to the rank of ambassador—James W. Riddleberger, Jacob D. Beam, and Hugh Cumming.

These and many others Gilbert coached and drilled with a nagging but loving paternalism. He sent them prowling the corridors of the League for the conclusive facts in the latest Balkan scandal to come before the delegates. He made them rewrite their reports and fussed with them over a word or phrase until he was sure that even the dimmest mind in the State Department could not miscontrue it. And when Saturday night came, he corralled them into a poker game and hectored them on every draw and bid with a kind of gleeful sadism.

The new vice-consul from Ceylon was given this treatment. Whatever he thought of it at first, he warmed to it in time. Looking back, Thompson considers Gilbert one of the strongest influences on his career.

Of course, life in Geneva had its gayer side. The lively American colony found ways to make life interesting for one of the few young bachelors among the diplomats. Pretty girls were always coming to town, and Tommy Thompson was not a man to let time drag heavily on their lovely hands.

In summer there were the Geneva beaches and parties in villas along the lake. In winter there was skiing, and Thompson ranged the Alps and the Juras, climbing the slopes before the days of the omnipresent ski lift with the *élan* of a mountain goat and taking his schusses on the descent with a wild abandon. And for a gambling man, as Thompson sometimes fancied himself, there was roulette or baccarat at the Evian casino on the French side of the lake or farther afield at Aix-les-Bains.

All these pursuits gave Thompson the reputation of a ladies' man (which he well deserved) and of a playboy (which he did not). The reputation may have hurt him in Washington. Or perhaps Prentiss Gilbert was too severe in his first efficiency reports on the new vice-consul. For whatever reason, the gods who ruled the Foreign Service from their dim nether world in Washington decided that Thompson should not be promoted. For six years he stood still while his contemporaries moved up.

The resulting disappointment must have created a conflict in his mind. Should he stay in the Foreign Service or should he pursue his earlier inclination to go into business? Not even his closest friends at the time were aware, however, of any bitterness on his part. He took on a bigger work load at the consulate, becoming the specialist on the International Labor Organization, which the United States joined in 1934, and sharing most of the political reporting with Jake Beam. In due course, the quality of his work was recognized and he was promoted to consul. Then, shortly before the outbreak of the war in 1939, he was transferred to the State Department and put in charge of Swiss and League of Nations affairs.

By this time, it might be said, he had served his apprenticeship as a Foreign Service officer. Among his colleagues the adjectives most frequently applied to him were "shrewd" and "sure-footed." Some of the higher officers of the Department, notably James C. Dunn, who was in charge of European affairs, were beginning to look on him as a possible "comer." In Geneva he had shown loyalty to his chiefs and to his service, perseverance in the face of disappointment, and aptitude for political reporting. All these qualities gave him the stamp of competence. Whether he would go beyond this and reach the level of excellence remained to be determined.

After two years in Washington, Thompson was transferred to the embassy in Moscow as second secretary and consul. In this job he was to succeed Charles E. Bohlen, one of the most promising young specialists in Soviet affairs. Thompson himself spoke no Russian and was in no sense a Soviet specialist. His assignment to Moscow was just one stage in the career of a Foreign Service officer, a career that might later reach its peak in Latin America or Western Europe.

He crossed the Pacific to avoid the war zone in Europe, where the British were standing alone against the Axis Powers, and arrived in Vladivostok in January, 1941.

Vladivostok in the Siberian winter looked like a town forgotten by everyone but the security police. From here it was eleven days to Moscow by the Trans-Siberian railway. The temperature outdoors ranged from forty to sixty degrees below zero. Somewhere in Siberia a steam line broke, and Thompson's car was left without heat for three days. The only way to keep warm was to stay in bed.

After that introduction to the country, Moscow almost looked good—even Stalin's Moscow. The dictator, enjoying a furtive flirtation with Hitler, was dreaming that he could stay out of the war while the Germans and the British fought each other to exhaustion. Of course, the agony of the Great Purge was still in the air, and officials of the government and even people in the street were nervous about talking to a foreigner. But the diplomatic corps, as Thompson found, was friendly and hospitable.

The American ambassador was Laurence Steinhardt, not a Foreign Service officer but a New York lawyer and loyal Democrat appointed by President Roosevelt. Thompson was made responsible for political reporting. This meant that he read translations of Soviet press reports and monitorings of broadcasts, picked up what information he could from other diplomats and any other sources, and tried to keep Washington informed of shifts and trends in Soviet foreign policy.

The false peace did not last long after Thompson's arrival. In June, Hitler struck at Russia. By October, when the first snow began to fly, his armies were threatening Moscow and his bombers were over the capital almost every night.

On October 15 Thompson called the American correspondents—there were about ten of them—to Spasso House, the Ambassador's residence, and told them they would have to leave by train that night, together with the embassy staff and other foreign diplomats and correspondents, for Kuibyshev on the Volga.

Thompson himself was to stay, however, and be responsible for the embassy. The third secretary, G. Frederick Reinhardt, and two American clerks were to stay with him. Thompson was also to represent British interests, because the British were subject to capture as belligerents and all of them were to leave.

Snow was falling that night in heavy flakes as the embassy cars, their headlights dimmed, crept away from Spasso House in the blackout. Off to the south and west the antiaircraft guns were thundering away, and at times the drone of a bomber throbbed through the din. On the great thoroughfare known as the B Circle army cars and trucks, with blue headlights tinting the snow, sped past in the opposite direction. Now and then fitful green flashes from the trolley wires lit up a labor battalion of men and women as they marched with spades on their shoulders to strengthen the city's defenses.

At the Kazan Station, crowded with Russian refugees and the fleeing diplomats, Thompson helped check off the thirty-two Americans who were leaving and to make sure that their food supplies and baggage were on board the train.

At half-past one in the morning the train eased its way out of Moscow. Amid the boom of the guns, Thompson drove slowly back to Spasso House.

He was now thirty-seven years old, this former janitor– ticket-agent–accountant–boarding-house-manager from Colorado, and he represented the power and majesty of the United States of America in the capital of the Soviets.

Power and majesty, however, were not negotiable items in the disorganized city. Even the police who maintained a perpetual vigil at the iron gates of Spasso House had fled. In the next few days only the ruthlessness of the regime prevented panic, with the mob violence, looting, destruction, and all that would have come with it.

But at this great turning point of the war, Washington had to be kept informed of the battle for Moscow. And messages from the United States government—some of them from President Roosevelt to Stalin—had to be delivered to the Soviet authorities.

Thompson at first had difficulty finding anyone in the Soviet government with whom he could keep in touch. He had better luck, however, in another direction. His Russian acquaintances were limited, but he found one man who began to give him tips on what was happening at the front—which towns had fallen to the Germans, which had been retaken by the Red army.

Thompson noted that these tips were borne out by later information, such as the official communiqués. This encouraged him to make use of his source, and enabled him to give Washington early and accurate reports on the great battle for Moscow long before such information came from the embassy staff in Kuibyshev or other intelligence sources.

He had begun, of course, the study of Russian, and he worked hard at it during this period—at the embassy, in air-raid shelters, and in occasional visits to the theater. His passion, however, was the ballet. Part of the Bolshoi company had stayed in Moscow, and it continued to give one ballet—*Swan Lake*—all through the war. Thompson actually saw 179 performances of *Swan Lake*. Even Tchaikovsky might have found that excessive. But perhaps the theater was warmer than Spasso House. Or perhaps it was good to mix with the crowd and try out his Russian during the intermissions. And, most likely, some of the ballerinas were young and pretty and glad to enjoy the company of the American diplomat.

The embassy staff returned from Kuibyshev in August, 1942, eight months after the United States entered the war. Thompson stayed on in Moscow two more years under two later ambassadors—Admiral William H. Standley and W. Averell Harriman.

For a time he hoped that the regime would mellow. At least, he thought, the war might have taught the Soviet leaders that they could trust their own people, for never had any people given their blood, sweat, and tears in such profusion.

But as the war went on and the Germans were turned back from Moscow, and then a year later from Stalingrad, he and his colleagues saw signs that Stalin had no intention of relaxing his iron rule when the victory was won. And from a source within the Soviet government—Maxim Litvinov, the former Ambassador to Washington and former commissar for foreign affairs—the embassy received a strong intimation that Stalin had no intention of continuing the wartime collaboration with the West once he felt safe without it.

Thompson left Moscow, then, in September, 1944, with no sunny illusions about the future of Soviet-American relations.

From his next post, as first secretary of the embassy in London, he made the rounds of the postwar conferences and saw in action most of the leaders and diplomats of the time—Truman, Churchill, Eden, Attlee, Bevin, Stalin, Molotov, Marshall, Stimson, and the rest.

His next stop was the State Department, where he became chief of the Division of Eastern European affairs in 1946, deputy director for European affairs in 1948, and a Deputy Assistant Secretary of State in 1949.

These were the years of the postwar disillusionment and of the first stern tests of will in the Cold War. Actually, as he said at the time, the term "Cold War" displeased him. It would be much better, he believed, for the nation to think of the conflict with international communism as a "Hundred Years' War." Americans were unfitted by temperament, he feared, for the protracted struggle that he saw in prospect. It was in the American tradition to believe that any problem could be solved by the right kind of man's going at it in the right kind of way. But the struggle forced upon us by the Russians offered no hope of quick or easy solution. Americans, he was certain, would have to curb their impatience and face up to a conflict that might last for generations—a conflict in which the political, moral, and economic resources and the social fabric of the nation would be severely tested.

Then forty-four and still a bachelor, Thompson sailed from New York on the *Saturnia* in June, 1948, for a conference in Rome. It was a happy, sunny voyage, and all the more so because he became acquainted on board ship with Mrs. Jane Monroe Goelet. She was the daughter of a research chemist in Winchester, Massachusetts, a young woman of abundant good looks and a warm, outgoing nature whose marriage had ended in divorce. Thompson saw to it that he met her again in Rome and then in other European cities. After their return to the United States, they were married in October, 1948.

Their first daughter, Jenny, was born in Washington in December, 1949; their second, Sherry, in Vienna in January, 1954. Mrs. Thompson's daughter by her earlier marriage, Fernanda Goelet, was also a member of their family and lived with them in their posts abroad until it was time for her to come back to school in America.

Their first foreign post after their marriage was Rome, where Thompson became minister-counselor in 1950. Two years later he was promoted to the rank of ambassador and made High Commissioner to Austria. This was to prove the making of his career.

In 1952, seven years after the end of the war, Austria was still an occupied country. As High Commissioner, Thompson had three roles. First, he argued and negotiated endlessly with the Russians in the Allied Control Council, of which the British and French were also members. Second, he dealt with the Austrian government on matters concerning Austria and the United States; for these purposes he ran what amounted to an embassy. Third, he ruled the American zone and sector; in this role he managed a radio station, newspaper, and even the plush Bristol Hotel in Vienna.

His first big challenge, however, and the first major test of his negotiating skill, came on a problem that only indirectly concerned Austria. In January, 1954, just two or three days after the birth of his daughter, Sherry, he left Vienna secretly for London to try to negotiate a settlement of the Trieste problem with representatives of Britain, Yugoslavia, and Italy.

Since the end of the war, the American and British armies had occupied the largely Italian-populated part of the Territory of Trieste, including the port, which was its most valuable asset. The Yugoslavs had occupied the rest. Now the Americans and British wanted to put an end to this divisive issue between Italy and Yugoslavia. If they could do so, they would remove the last acute trouble spot on the entire southern flank of the NATO alliance running from the Atlantic to the Black Sea.

The London talks opened in secret, with the Italians left outside. Thompson and the principal delegates of Britain and Yugoslavia were backed by teams of political and military advisers. The Italians came in only at the end. Day after day the three delegations sat in plenary session while formal, repetitive speeches were made by the Yugoslavs.

This was Thompson's first prolonged exposure to the kind of negotiating tactics he was to encounter again and again in later dealings with the Russians. It was also his first chance to display the dogged patience and ingenuity that were to become his trade-marks. He listened to the Yugoslav speeches, trying to note changes in emphasis and inflection. Then, after unnumbered sessions, he suggested that the three principals get together in an informal way. They met at the house of Vladimir Velebit, the Yugoslav, and the first talks were so promising that the negotiators dismissed most of their waiting advisers. Still, Velebit, on instructions from Belgrade, had to go on repeating his position like a litany. It was a trying business, but Thompson held on, trying to sense the moment and the combination of proposals that would make an agreement possible. At last, in October, after eight months of talks, he was able to put forward a new "formula," and agreement was reached.

The agreement gave the part of Trieste occupied by the British and Americans to Italy and the rest to the Yugoslavs. It laid down safeguards for the use of the port by both countries and disposed of other points that had caused difficulty. The Trieste infection was removed from the Adriatic area.

On several occasions the Russians had said they would not sign an Austrian peace treaty until Trieste was out of the way. At other times they had said they would not do it until there was a peace treaty with Germany. Whatever the pretext, they seemed determined to exploit the economic resources of their zone of Austria as long as they could and to keep a military outpost in south-central Europe.

In February, 1955, however, a few months after the Trieste settlement, they began to put out hints that they would sign an Austrian treaty if union with Germany were forbidden and guarantees were given that Austria would never become a hostile military base.

More than 350 negotiating sessions had already been held between the West and the Soviets on the details of an Austrian treaty. Consequently, there was no certainty of success when Thompson sat down with the Soviet, British, French, and Austrian representatives in Vienna on May 2 to make one more effort.

What followed was probably the most intensive burst of negotiation since the end of the war. In eleven day-and-night sessions, which brought the total to 379, Thompson lost eighteen pounds.

The big sticking point was the quantity of oil and other economic loot the Soviets would take from Austria, and how it would be extracted. The Austrians themselves were so anxious to get rid of the Russians that Thompson had to bear the burden of their defense. So hard did he fight to protect their interests that the Russians accused him of being "more royal than the king."

In particular, he insisted that the clauses on the reparations should be part of the treaty and not set apart, as the Soviets wanted, in a direct agreement between the Soviet Union and Austria. If these clauses were part of the treaty, he reasoned, the United States, Britain, and France would have a legal basis for coming to the aid of Austria if a dispute later arose over their fulfilment.

The deadline set for the signature of the treaty was May 15. As this date approached, Thompson tried one more formula that would retain the detailed economic clauses in the treaty itself. After a night of suspense, the Soviets agreed, and the treaty was signed on May 15, 1955.

Austria recovered her freedom. For the first time since the immediate postwar period, the Red army withdrew from occupied territory. It was a genuine success for the West. Coming after the Trieste settlement, it confirmed Thompson's reputation as a tireless and resourceful negotiator, a diplomat who could fathom the ways of the inscrutable Communists and wait them out at the bargaining table.

The next year his work in aiding the Hungarian refugees who poured into Austria when the Red army suppressed the Hungarian revolution won him even higher regard in Washington. In the spring of 1957, when it came time for President Eisenhower to appoint a new ambassador to the Soviet Union to succeed Charles Bohlen, he was the obvious man.

The Thompsons arrived in Moscow on July 10, 1957. The atmosphere was not promising. The government and people of the United States had not forgotten the brutal suppression of the Hungarian revolution the year before. The Soviets were still denouncing the "Eisenhower Doctrine"—the intention proclaimed by the President to resist any overt Communist aggression in the Middle East.

Both countries were pressing on with their tests of nuclear weapons—a problem that was to give trouble all through Thompson's tour of duty in Moscow. Premier Bulganin and Nikita Khrushchev, the Communist Party secretary, had been threatening the European allies and neutrals with atomic destruction if they allowed the United States to use bases on their soil. The Soviets were also watching uneasily the increasing cohesion of the West: the European Common Market had been born that year and the first three German divisions had been put under NATO command.

In the Soviet Union itself, the aggressive and cunning Khrushchev, who had recently told American newspapermen that their grandchildren would live under socialism, had come out on top in the power struggle that followed Stalin's death. Only a week before Thompson's arrival, the leaders of the "anti-party group"—Viacheslav Molotov, Georgi Malenkov, Lazar Kaganovitch, and others—had been cast out of the party leadership.

Once again, as in 1940, Thompson moved into a spot left vacant by his close friend Charles E. Bohlen, who had been ambassador since 1953.

This did not make the job any less awesome. "Chip" Bohlen had chosen to be a specialist on the Soviet Union almost from the moment he entered the service in 1929. One of the undoubted stars of the diplomatic world, he had the profile and the presence of a Barrymore and a wit that was almost too sharp for his own good. His Russian was so assured that he did not hesitate to negotiate in that language. And he loved nothing better than to argue with the argumentative Russians, poking a finger into a commissar's chest and confounding him with an apt quotation from Chekhov or a choice bit of hokum from the scriptures of the sainted Lenin.

The Soviet hierarchy respected him and seemed to have confidence that he faithfully and accurately reported their views to Washington.

In contrast, Thompson had become a Soviet specialist by accident. Persuasive in English—though even in this he was less articulate than Bohlen—he could not hope to achieve Bohlen's mastery of Russian. He was also by nature more quiet and withdrawn. Though he could hold his own in argument with the Russians, he never sailed into them in public with the happy abandon of his predecessor.

And at the start he was rather concerned when he sensed that the Soviet leaders wondered whether he would be as accurate a reporter of their words as Bohlen had been. In Washington, the State Department had a parallel worry: Was Mikhail Menshikov, the Soviet Ambassador, reporting his conversations accurately to Moscow, or was he saying what he thought Moscow might like to hear? Menshikov never lived down this suspicion. Thompson did, and eventually achieved a relationship of such confidence with the Soviet leaders as no American diplomat had ever before enjoyed.

Bohlen had been on good terms with the foreign correspondents in Moscow. He held a weekly meeting with the American reporters as a group and often saw them individually. He talked freely, drawing on his previous experience in the Soviet Union and his knowledge of Russian history and literature. The correspondents liked it, though when they wrote their stories they usually found that Bohlen had given nothing away.

Thompson, on the other hand, met the press at first with the wariness of a matador facing a killer bull. Of course, even his colleagues in the foreign service had found him tight-lipped. He continued the weekly meetings, however, and the reporters generally grew to like and respect him for giving them information that would make the situation more understandable. And Thompson soon learned that it was better to have accurate news reaching the American reader than the tainted stuff that was only too available to every correspondent in Moscow.

He never consciously misled a newspaperman. And though he never was guilty of "leaks," he often gave the kind of guidance that took a reporter off a false scent and put him on the right one.

Bohlen was so eminent in his field that he had awed his staff. He had full confidence in his own judgment and had made his reports to Washington very much his own. He was intuitive. Some of his hunches in the Stalin era were celebrated. In 1949 he had sensed from a newspaper interview that Stalin was ready to lift the Berlin blockade, and this insight had paid off.

More recently, however, some of his staff and some of the specialists in the State Department had felt that his political antennae might have been missing some signals. He had been slow, they thought, in recognizing the emergence of Khrushchev from the "collective leadership" that followed Stalin's death.

Thompson was much more cautious, more analytical. The members of his staff found that he listened to them, particularly on domestic trends and developments within the Soviet Union. If their reasoning impressed him, the dispatches that went to Washington reflected it. This pleased the staff.

On Soviet foreign policy Thompson acted with more assurance. One of the better Moscow correspondents says that after little more than a year as ambassador his ability to detect shifts or significant departures in Soviet foreign policy was "absolutely uncanny."

Members of the staff and the newspapermen who played poker at the embassy called Bohlen a hunch-player, Thompson a much more cautious odds-player. Neither of them, however, ever won enough to require a declaration in his income tax returns.

*

With so reticent a man, it is hard to determine exactly what Thompson conceived his mission to be and what he thought he might accomplish. Even after leaving Moscow he was wary about showing his hand, perhaps because he thought he might again be called upon to negotiate with the Soviets in a crisis or at some major turning point.

Certain themes, however, run through the little he has said publicly and privately over the years.

Anything that tends to make Soviet society a more "normal" society, he thinks, is something to be welcomed by the West. In the long run it is good if the standard of living goes up and the terror goes down. A rising standard of living will stimulate the "revolution of rising expectations" that is making itself felt in so many parts of the world. A reduction of the terror will encourage discussion, a more critical view of Soviet institutions, a more widespread awareness of what other countries have that the Soviet Union does not have.

It is also to our advantage, he is convinced, to open as many doors as we can between the Soviet Union and the rest of the world. The West has much to gain and little to lose in every kind of exchange—cultural, technical, scientific, or the mere flow of tourists. The exchange program that began in 1958 is, he is sure, one of the best things that has ever happened in Soviet-American relations.

"Exchanges of all kinds are extremely helpful," he says. "I know we can't measure the effects, but we will never have a stable basis for our relations until we know each other. Whether we are going to be friends or enemies, it is a good thing to know each other."

This line of thought probably contributed to his certainty that Khrushchev was a man to be cultivated—both by himself as an ambassador and by the leaders of the West. Khrushchev, with his earthy ways, his peasant shrewdness, his political flair, knew what the Soviet people were feeling and thinking, and he knew that their wants and desires could not be eternally suppressed. And Khrushchev, as Thompson saw him, had the stature and the foresight to move—to ease the terror, to open the doors and windows at least a little.

Not that Thompson found Khrushchev less fanatical a Communist than any of the other leaders; he was simply more sensitive to what in other countries is called public opinion, and more of a realist in facing up to what had to be done.

Given the frightful power now held by the United States and the Soviet Union, Thompson believes that it is good to "keep talking." He himself contrived to keep talking to the Soviet leaders even when relations between the two governments were about as bad as could be. Undoubtedly his experience in the Trieste and Austrian settlements led him in this direction.

"Given our different approaches to every sort of question," he says, "enormous misunderstandings are bound to exist. We should constantly try to reduce the misunderstandings by normal diplomatic dialogue."

His belief in the efficacy of talk led him to be more sanguine than many of his colleagues in Washington about meetings with the Soviets.

Whether Thompson ever believed that it might be possible to negotiate a broad settlement of differences with the

Soviets cannot be determined. It seems fairly sure, however, that after several years in Moscow he did not believe it was possible to reach *fundamental* agreements with this generation of Soviet leaders—that is, agreements that would mean the abandonment of their urge to remake the world in their own image. On the other hand, the Trieste and Austrian settlements taught him that patience, perseverance, and good timing might bring about agreement on specific issues—say, on Berlin or on nuclear testing.

Thompson's role as ambassador and the validity of the "keep talking" approach cannot be evaluated without taking into account the fact that this approach has its opponents in the United States and other countries of the Atlantic alliance. It is hard to identify the opponents in the foggy anonymity of the State Department. But outside the Department the most forceful critic of the "keep talking" approach has been Dean Acheson, Secretary of State under President Truman and an occasional adviser to President Kennedy.

As those on the Acheson side of the argument see it, American foreign policy has been thrown out of kilter by the "Kremlinologists." The focus of American policy, they contend, should be not on the Soviet Union but on Western Europe and Germany—particularly on Germany. The United States should use its superior power to hold the Soviets at arm's length while it ties Germany irrevocably into the Western alliance. It should work to build an Atlantic partnership so strong that the Communist bloc will never be able to menace it, so prosperous that the Communist countries will pale beside it, so rich in skills and resources that the uncommitted nations will inevitably choose to hitch their wagons to it.

The "flirtations" with the Soviets, in this view, frustrate the attainment of this supreme objective. They arouse suspicions among the allies: Are the Americans going to make a "deal" with the Russians and leave Europe to its fate? They trouble the Germans, annoy the French, stimulate the British to seek their own special relationship with Moscow, tempt the Japanese to talk and trade with the Communists. Thus the "keep talking" approach, in the Acheson view, serves the Soviets more than it does the West because it increases the strains in the Atlantic alliance and among the nations of the free world.

It may take several generations to find out who is right. It must be borne in mind, however, that Thompson was not making his own policy in Moscow but was following instructions approved both by President Eisenhower and President Kennedy. And, given the nature of his orders, even his critics concede that he carried them out with unusual skill.

In the five years of Thompson's tour of duty—a longer period than that of any American ambassador before him —the Soviets sent up "Sputnik," the first artificial earth satellite, put a man in orbit, and sent a rocket to the moon.

In those five years Vice-President Nixon made his sensational visit to the Soviet Union and met Khrushchev in the celebrated "kitchen debate" at the American exhibition. This was only one of many trying moments in the visit for the ambassador who was Nixon's guide and mentor.

The following year it was Khrushchev's turn to visit America, to travel from coast to coast, to meet President Eisenhower at Camp David. Thompson went along, and again there were moments when the ulcer that has plagued him throughout his career almost laid him low.

Then there was the U-2 incident—the shooting down of an American reconnaissance plane inside the Soviet Union. And for most of the five years there was Berlin, with Khrushchev demanding that the Western allies get out, and the allies refusing to get out. In most of this fencing and maneuvering Thompson played a part, and toward the end of his tour he was elected to carry on, alone, a continuing probe of Soviet aims and intentions.

Finally, there was Cuba, a growing irritant in Soviet-American relations and one that was to reach the point of crisis when Thompson had moved to an advisory post in Washington.

Perhaps Thompson's most unusual achievement during his Moscow assignment was the relationship he established and maintained with Premier Khrushchev. The Premier, the first Deputy Premier Anastas Mikoyan, and other men prominent in the hierarchy usually came to the receptions at the different embassies on their national days, as well as to the government receptions in the Kremlin.

Many diplomats swarmed around Khrushchev on these occasions, trying to talk to him or hear what he was saying. Thompson held aloof, especially at the start. After a while, Khrushchev would ask where he was and then cross the room to greet him. The other diplomats would then hold back, giving Thompson a chance to talk privately to

Khrushchev. These fortuitous meetings often gave Thompson a hint of the way Soviet policy was moving.

Jane Thompson made her own way with the Soviet leaders. She had acquired a kind of free-style Russian, and she did not shrink from engaging Mikoyan or Khrushchev himself in argument. At times Thompson seemed nervous about her frankness, but the Russians took it well. On several occcasions the Khrushchev family entertained the Thompson family in the country and the Premier took the Thompson girls for a sleigh ride. Courtesies such as these and so many opportunities for informal talk had never before been given to a non-Communist diplomat.

This relationship did not occur because Thompson humored Khrushchev. And no critic at home ever accused him of "appeasement." He had his instructions and he carried them out, and usually they were unsatisfactory from the Soviet point of view. But he was able, nevertheless, to do what every diplomat would like to be able to do—establish a line of access to the center of power and keep it open. Even the U-2 incident did not break this line of access.

On May 5, 1960, Thompson went to the Kremlin to observe a meeting of the Supreme Soviet. According to protocol, he should have taken his customary seat in the second box of the hall. However, an attendant insisted that he was to sit in the first box. Suspecting something, he entered the first box but sat in the rear where he could not be seen from the floor.

His instinct was right. In an angry speech Khrushchev denounced the United States for trying to wreck the "summit conference," which was to open in Paris on May 16, by committing "aggressive acts." American aircraft had been flying over the Soviet Union, he said, and on May 1 one of them had actually been shot down over Soviet territory.

In Washington the government had already announced that a U-2 high-altitude plane engaged on a "weather mission" in the Middle East had disappeared. Then, following a "cover plan" prepared in advance, it said that if the plane had in fact flown over the Soviet Union, the intrusion must have been accidental.

In Moscow, Thompson had gone that same night to an embassy reception. There he learned from someone that the Soviets had captured an American pilot and were holding him. He hurried back to the American Embassy and sent an urgent message to Washington. But the cover story had already been issued.

On May 7 Khrushchev sprang the trap and exposed the American lie. He announced that the U-2 had been shot down far inside the Soviet Union; that it had carried high-altitude cameras and other equipment for espionage purposes; that the pilot, Francis Gary Powers, had been captured; and that he had freely admitted that he had been on a reconnaissance mission that was to have taken him from Pakistan to Norway, straight across the Soviet Union.

In Washington two days later, the Secretary of State, Christian Herter, conceded the accuracy of this account. Khrushchev, nevertheless, tried to absolve Eisenhower. He was sure, he said, that the President could not have known about this espionage. But Eisenhower himself on May 11 —just five days before the Paris conference—took personal responsibility for the U-2 flights and intimated that Soviet secrecy made them necessary.

In the meantime Thompson had encountered Khrushchev at a reception given by the Czechoslovak embassy. Contrary to his earlier custom, he went straight to the Premier and greeted him. Khrushchev took him aside and talked of the damage done to Soviet-American relations.

Later, speaking to the crowd of diplomats and officials, Khrushchev bitterly denounced the perfidy of the United States and Norway. But he absolved Thompson and said he was sure the Ambassador did not know about the flights. And, giving a toast, he clinked glasses with Thompson and said: "Here's hoping we never clink anywhere else."

At a Kremlin reception several months later, the Premier showed that the U-2 incident was still on his mind by going back to it in a conversation with the Ambassador and Mrs. Thompson. To make his point he stepped on Thompson's foot and said:

"If I do that to you, I ought to apologize. Your government ought to have apologized."

Thompson replied that the Soviet government kept fleets of trawlers off the American coast and carried on other kinds of espionage. As a crowd began to gather around them Khrushchev said:

"Maybe it was Mrs. Thompson's fault—women are always starting something."

"Yes, it was all my fault," said Mrs. Thompson, "and let's not talk about it any more."

The Premier agreed.

Three or four months before this, on May 16, Khrushchev had confronted Eisenhower at the Paris conference and demanded that the United States condemn and cancel all flights over the Soviet Union and punish the guilty. He also told the President that he would not be permitted to make his scheduled visit to the Soviet Union the following month.

Thompson witnessed this humiliation. It seemed to mean the undoing of nearly three years' effort to keep the two sides talking to each other. Still, it did not blight his faith in face-to-face diplomacy. It was he, as much as anyone, who persuaded President Kennedy to meet Premier Khrushchev in Vienna in June, 1961.

No explosion occurred at that meeting. But the young President, still smarting from the failure of the hare-brained attempt in April to invade Cuba with a small force of exiles, was given a rough time by Khrushchev, particularly on the Berlin issue. The President did not enjoy the experience, but he did not hold it against the Ambassador.

When Thompson's long tour in Moscow came to an end and he returned to the United States in the summer of 1962, he was made Ambassador at Large and given special responsibility for relations with the Soviets. In this role he again succeeded Bohlen, who had been appointed Ambassador to France. When Bohlen left for Paris in October, just at the moment when Soviet missile and bomber bases were discovered in Cuba, it was to Thompson that President Kennedy turned for judgments that inevitably carried with them the awesome possibilities of nuclear war.

Though he was then recovering from a serious operation, Thompson played his full part in the ten days of almost continuous meetings at the White House and the State Department. In retrospect, some of the other participants put him high in the group of Presidential advisers that included the Attorney General, Robert F. Kennedy; the Secretary of State, Dean Rusk; the Secretary of Defense, Robert S. McNamara; the Director of the Central Intelligence Agency, John A. McCone, and the Presidential assistant for national security affairs, McGeorge Bundy.

Before the American people and the rest of the world knew about the Soviet missile and bomber bases in Cuba, this group faced questions like these: Should the United States invade Cuba? Should it knock out the bases with an air strike? If so, should previous warning be given? Should the President order an air and sea blockade of Cuba to cut off the delivery of more missiles, bombers, and nuclear warheads? What would be the Soviet reaction to each of these moves? And what would be the risk of provoking nuclear war?

Thompson's preliminary advice was that the United States should avoid any hasty action that would cause Khrushchev to take precipitate counteraction. The first steps on the American side, Thompson argued, should leave Khrushchev time to reflect and consult his advisers. An invasion or air strike, without some kind of previous move, might cause the Russians to react with violence against West Berlin or the American bases in Turkey. In line with this argument, Thompson, in common with some of the other advisers, favored a blockade. But the blockade, he said, should be backed up by military preparations that would leave Khrushchev in no doubt of the President's determination to order an invasion or air strike if that should become necessary.

As the idea of a blockade gained favor with the President, Thompson pressed a collateral argument. The more legal the American action could be made to appear to the world, he said, the greater would be the probability of Soviet acceptance. And if some kind of international approval could be obtained—such as an endorsement of the blockade by the Organization of American States—the probability of such acceptance would be further strengthened.

On the night of October 22, President Kennedy announced that he would impose an air and sea blockade to prevent further deliveries of missiles and bombers to Cuba, and he called on Khrushchev to withdraw the offensive weapons already there. The next day, the Council of the Organization of American States, by a vote of 19 to 0, authorized the use of force to support the blockade. This unanimous action apparently surprised the Soviets. Together with support for the blockade from the NATO allies, it helped to account for the hesitancy in Soviet countermoves during the next few days.

On the day the blockade was imposed, twenty-five Soviet ships were approaching Cuba. Inevitably, President Kennedy put the question to Thompson:

"Will those ships turn around, or will they try to run the blockade?"

Thompson's considered reply was that the Russians would probably try to send one ship through the blockade —perhaps for reasons of prestige. But the other Soviet ships—those carrying the missiles and bombers—would probably turn back.

It was one of the shrewdest judgments he had ever made. On the second day of the blockade a Soviet tanker did enter the blockade zone. After a perfunctory check, the Navy allowed it to proceed to Cuba—a sign that the United States did not intend to humiliate the Soviets any more than was necessary. The next day a dozen or more Soviet ships, those believed to be carrying incriminating cargoes, altered course and turned away from the blockade area.

Then the President put another question to Thompson: Would the Soviets dismantle the missile bases in Cuba and withdraw the missiles? Thompson said he believed they would.

For the next seventy-two hours, messages went back and forth from Washington to the Kremlin. During those seventy-two hours, the United States made every kind of military move to indicate its readiness to invade Cuba and cope with the consequences, nuclear or otherwise. And then, on October 28, Khrushchev sent word that the missiles would be withdrawn.

Another big question remained: Would the Soviets also withdraw their bombers from Cuba? Some of the President's advisers thought they would not. But Thompson said they would, and he said it with some certainty. There was no point, he reasoned, in keeping the bombers there after the missiles had been withdrawn. Several weeks of maneuvering and talking were necessary, but in the end Khrushchev withdrew the bombers.

By the time the crisis was over, Thompson had become, in the words of one White House adviser, "the President's No. 1 boy on Soviet affairs." Seldom, if ever, had an officer of the Foreign Service made such a place for himself in Washington in so short a time.

Not long after the Cuban crisis, when Thompson was

able to relax for a few moments, a friend asked him what he thought of the Foreign Service after all his experience.

"You probably remember," said Thompson, "that in my college days I once thought of going into business—perhaps the importing-exporting business. Well, one day while I was still in Geneva I talked about a job to the vice-president in charge of one of our biggest exporting companies.

"He was a kind of harassed-looking man, and while he was talking I wondered what he hoped to get out of life. So I asked him what he wanted to do when he retired. He said he thought he would like to come to Europe and do something that would get him in touch with interesting people—something on the fringes of government so he could meet people in the embassies and foreign offices. While he was telling me this, I began to realize that he was working all his life to get just a little of what I already had. At that time I could go over to the League of Nations almost any day and talk to Litvinov or Eden or some of the other foreign ministers and diplomats. It was just part of my daily routine to meet 'interesting people.' "

But being in the Foreign Service, he went on, meant a great deal more than this. During his years in the State Department and in missions abroad, he had met many talented businessmen who had entered government service. This service, despite all its frustrations, had given them a sense of purpose such as they had never experienced in the world of commerce and industry. Once having been in government, they were never again completely satisfied with private enterprise and its rewards.

As for himself, Thompson said, his years in the Foreign

Service had enabled him to participate in the making of history, in the effort to meet the great issues and challenges of our times. Surely, it would be hard to choose a career that offered higher rewards than this.

Sterling B. Hendricks

AT THE PINNACLE OF PLANT SCIENCE

GOVE HAMBIDGE

THE TRUSTEES OF
PRINCETON UNIVERSITY

BY VIRTUE OF THE AUTHORITY VESTED IN THEM

UNDER A PROGRAM INITIATED BY JOHN D. ROCKEFELLER 3RD

TO STRENGTHEN THE CAREER

SERVICE IN THE FEDERAL GOVERNMENT

DO HEREBY GRANT A

ROCKEFELLER PUBLIC SERVICE AWARD

TO

STERLING BROWN HENDRICKS

IN RECOGNITION OF DISTINGUISHED SERVICE

TO THE GOVERNMENT OF THE UNITED STATES

AND TO THE AMERICAN PEOPLE

PRESIDENT

CLERK

DONE IN NASSAU HALL
PRINCETON, NEW JERSEY

STERLING B. HENDRICKS

A skeleton can tell you only a little about the man it occupied, and the same is true of the usual Who's Who type of skeletonized biography. From the brief biographical sketch of Sterling Hendricks we learn that he has been a scientist in the Bureau of Plant Industry of the United States Department of Agriculture for thirty-five years, and Chief Scientist since 1948, and that he holds at least six awards for high scientific achievement and public service —the Hoblitzelle award (shared with his co-worker, H. A. Borthwick) of $10,000 for the most outstanding recent accomplishment in agriculture, the Rockefeller Public Service Award, the award of the President of the United States for distinguished federal service, the Day medal of the Geological Society of America, the scientific award of the Washington Academy of Sciences, and the Hillebrand prize of the American Chemical Society. We learn that he is a member of the National Academy of Sciences and a number of distinguished scientific societies; studied at the University of Arkansas, the Kansas State Agricultural College, and the California Institute of Technology, where he got his Ph.D. in 1926; married Edith Ochiltree in 1931; and was born in Elysian Fields, Texas, in 1902. We also learn that he is an expert mountain climber and belongs to the American and Canadian Alpine Clubs and the Appalachian Mountain Club.

What we do not learn from the biography is that Sterling Hendricks is one of the world's truly great agricultural scientists. The awards he has received represent the evaluative judgments of his peers, some of whom consider him the most outstanding agricultural scientist today. But the name of Sterling Hendricks means nothing to the general public. It is not attached to any spectacular new product or process or associated with some dramatic difference of opinion on a public issue. His field has been what is called basic or "pure" research, the kind of thing Faraday was doing in 1831 when he generated an electric current in the laboratory by rotating a copper disk between two poles of a horseshoe magnet—a matter of purely theoretical interest, which he could hardly foresee would be the foundation of our modern huge electrical industry. Or the Dutchman Leeuwenhoek, perhaps, looking through a magnifying glass at a blob of saliva and finding it full of strange little beasts—the beginning of modern bacteriology, with all that it means to human welfare.

The examples could be vastly multiplied. It is perhaps enough to say that there would be no modern medicine, no airplanes, no electronic devices, no astronauts hurtling weightlessly through space, if it were not for the discovery of basic facts and principles by scientists who may be unknown to most of us, though well known to other scientists.

Hendricks is one of this breed of avid seekers after knowledge. That he has been able to stick to basic research throughout his career is in itself a mark of exceptional ability and singleness of purpose. The pressure of budget-conscious administrators and legislators has generally been in the other direction: toward practical or applied experiment. A great deal of progress has been made through this kind of experiment. But the time has come when agricultural science must put more emphasis on basic research if it is to advance as medical science has done. Basic research cannot be hurried. Its results may not be immediately useful. But it is an essential investment in the future for any highly developed industry or nation.

Few men have seen this need as clearly as Hendricks, and fewer still have exemplified it so consistently and brilliantly.

Now about the mountain climbing.

A man's life is one piece. He shows the same traits and attitudes and interests in his extracurricular activities as in his work—sometimes more revealingly or in sharper outline. Thus it may be useful, though unorthodox, to begin with this aspect of Sterling Hendricks' life.

Hendricks is a rather stocky, square-rigged, muscular person, obviously adaptable to hard outdoor exercise and with a taste for it that I am sure he cannot fully satisfy. How can an able research scientist get anything much in the way of recreation? Throughout his career Hendricks has had to put in about seventy hours of work a week (a little less in recent years), including the laboratory and the prodigious volume of reading needed to keep up to date in a number of rapidly developing fields. This is roughly equivalent to a twelve-hour day six days a week, year in, year out.

Not much time left for recreation; but to create, one needs to re-create. Hendricks re-creates by managing a sizable garden; by nonprofessional reading, which I shall mention later; and by spending his month's vacation every year climbing mountains (and planning the expeditions in advance and savoring them afterward). He is one of those people you sometimes see from a distance or in photographs crawling up the face of a rock like a fly on the kitchen wall.

Mountain climbing is hard and dangerous work. (Hard, Hendricks agrees, but not so dangerous.) Why does a man go back summer after summer, about thirty of them now, to those remote Canadian mountains with a little group of like-minded cronies, trekking unexplored wilderness, toting up to 125 pounds on his back, scaling sharp inclines with rope and piton and ice ax, sleeping on frosty stone, sucking oxygen-thin air into his lungs?

Hendricks started this in his student days in California, when he walked the full length of naturalist John Muir's trail, from Mount Whitney to Yosemite in the High Sierras, in 1924. He has been at it ever since, mostly in British Columbia; today, probably no one knows the wild interior of that province as intimately as he.

The fascination? Perhaps contrast; a man who spends his working life doing such things as measuring the invisible distances between invisible atoms in an invisible molecule might well turn to a mountain for relief. Perhaps the challenge of verticality, man against mountain, mind against mass. Perhaps love of exploring wilderness that no human being may ever have seen before. (Most of Hendricks' scientific work has been the exploration of unvisited areas of knowledge.) Perhaps the reward of magnificent views achieved by a hard climb. (When Hendricks talks about scientific research you get this same sense of wide vistas.) Perhaps the challenge to skill and judgment posed by a difficult ascent, when you appraise the terrain meticulously in advance and, if the chance of success appears reasonable, proceed step by step as the way opens. (This is also how research is done.) Perhaps the combination of self-reliance and teamwork as you advance independently yet roped together, mutually responsible, mutually confident of one another. (Hendricks' research has all been such self-reliant teamwork.)

His ascent of Mount McKinley was not recreation, however, but a World War II undertaking. This is the highest peak in North America, 20,300 feet, and it had been climbed only twice before. The United States Quartermaster Corps, in cooperation with other United States and Canadian military units, sent an expedition there in 1942 to test many kinds of field equipment—clothing, footwear, tents, sleeping bags, cooking utensils, processed foods, and so on—in actual use under extreme weather conditions. The project anticipated the possible need for a northern invasion of Japan. Hendricks was requisitioned as scientist and seasoned mountaineer to participate in the anonymous, successful work.

Fifteen summers later, in August, 1957, he was on another expedition in which the mountain almost bested the man. This was on Mount Howson, in British Columbia. His companions were Major Rex Gibson, then president of the Alpine Club of Canada; Donald Hubbard, physicist of the United States Bureau of Standards; Alexander Fabergé, geneticist of the University of Texas; and Alvin Peterson, engineer with the United States Ordnance Laboratory. (If you are one of those who thinks scientists are soft-handed eggheads, please note this list. All were veteran mountain climbers.) Fabergé and Peterson stayed at base camp. The other three ascended: Gibson in the lead, cutting footholds in the hard snow, Hubbard next, Hendricks last, as anchor man. Suddenly Gibson toppled, hit on the head by a falling rock. The other two tried desperately to hold. Then all three, tied together on the nylon line, tumbled in a tangled mass down the icy slope. They stopped abruptly; they had broken through the crust at a point where it was undermined by a small stream of water, just short of a sheer drop of 500 feet.

Gibson was unconscious. Hubbard had a broken leg and could not walk; Hendricks, a broken shoulder, broken ribs, a fractured spine. But he could walk, after a fashion. He undertook the slow, agonized descent for help; at one point, letting himself down a steep declivity, the rope snagged and he had to pull it loose with his teeth, since shoulder and spine were badly crippled. Darkness came. He sat out the night, not daring to doze. Next day, after

more painful progress, he finally wrapped the eighty-foot
rope around his body and slid down the glacier, with the
rope acting as a brake. He got to camp, and Fabergé and
Peterson left him there and went up for the other two.
They brought Hubbard down. Gibson was dead.

Eric Hutton wrote a vivid account of this expedition
for *Maclean's Magazine,* calling it "one of the most remarkable episodes—an episode at once tragic and trium-
phant—in all the eventful annals of the supremely dangerous sport of mountain climbing."

(But the fact remains, says Hendricks, that in hundreds
of climbs this was the only serious accident he ever had.
His wife and daughter vacation less strenuously on Cape
Cod.)

As a youngster in Louisiana, with the Gulf and the Mississippi near by, Hendricks was a long-distance swimmer.
For a number of years after coming to Washington, he
swam in the Potomac River, from just below Great Falls
down to Glen Echo. I know the stretches below and above
Great Falls rather well; I used to slide along them in a
kayak every week end: a lovely place, with much fast
water and frequent rapids, well known for a tendency to
drown people. Hendricks did not think of it as dangerous,
just challenging. The river is so gelatinous, he says, that
you can swim with your body half out of water, using the
"Potomac crawl" to beat away the sewage with one hand.
Also, you go in only at high water, when the rocks are
well covered; the water acts as a cushion to keep you
away from them. In rapids, the trick is to swim feet first
so you don't risk striking your head and being knocked
out. But don't go in just below the falls; the turbid water

there is full of air, and it won't hold you up. The only real difficulty is getting caught in a whirlpool occasionally. Then you have a fight on your hands.

I prefer a kayak.

I think this intrepidness—shall we call it?—would make Hendricks a hard man to control against his will and may have something to do with his independence; and this confidence in the face of even very hazardous problems— in fact, this zest in seeking them—has something to do with his success in basic research.

His extracurricular reading is also characteristic. Like many scientists (he said), he was practically a cultural illiterate when he got his Ph.D., knowing a great deal about mathematics, physics, and chemistry but precious little about anything else; he had taken only one college course in English and one in history. Someone apparently suggested that this was intellectually rather deplorable; at any rate, he decided that do-it-yourself culture might be as good as the college brand and set himself a course of nonprofessional reading, which he has kept up ever since. For one thing, he has read the Manchester *Guardian* assiduously for forty years—in itself a liberal education that probably few physical chemists get. He also reads the *Saturday Review* regularly and likes John Ciardi; I don't know whether this is typical of physical chemists. He has read much or most of the many-volume Oxford *Ancient History,* and currently is immersed in the Dark Ages, which in some ways are exceptionally luminous. He is an economic liberal.

How many culturally educated but scientifically illiterate people would go to the same trouble to close their intellectual gaps?

A lively mind, in short, interested no less in the world than in the atom. My guess is that this breadth of view might have a salutary influence on a man's research. The old Greeks were like that, and they pioneered in science as well as in other things. Hippocrates wrote, of medicine: "Life is short and Art is long; the Crisis is fleeting, Experiment risky, Decision difficult." Asclepiades taught an atomic or corpuscular theory of disease. It is not a bad thing, nowadays, for a scientist to have a deep concern, as Hendricks has, for fostering the values of civilization.

Hendricks probably started with a predilection for the agricultural aspects of science because his father owned a plantation, inherited from *his* father, in Elysian Fields in eastern Texas. The fields were elysian only in name. Hendricks' grandfather had been ruined by the Civil War; the father was a physician, but most people in the little town were poor and he had to farm to supplement his income. Like other boys, young Hendricks was plowing behind a mule at the age of twelve. He was also visiting patients with his father, developing an interest in medicine and a humanitarian viewpoint. To get better schooling, he went to live with relatives in Shreveport, Louisiana. Then college in Arkansas, where he worked his way by clerking in the bookstore; then Kansas State; then itinerant jobs in the Midwest to earn some money; then Caltech, which already had a notable reputation, under Robert A. Millikan, for training in chemistry and physics—exclusively.

An exciting place, Hendricks says, where you felt the stir of new knowledge, as people must have felt it in ancient Athens. Besides, he was young, and the 1920's were a decade of supreme confidence in the future—one's own and mankind's—the interlude between the World War (doubtless the last), and the world depression (unforeseen).

In 1928 he came to work in F. G. Cottrell's famous Fixed Nitrogen Laboratory, in the Agriculture Department's Bureau of Chemistry and Soils.

While Hendricks was a student and in the early days of his career, the United States was just beginning to do big things in the chemical industry. It was stimulated partly by the wartime loss of chemical imports from Germany, which it now had to produce for itself; partly by the development of synthetic fibers (rayon, for example) and plastics; partly by the perfecting by Cottrell of a practical process for making nitrate fertilizer, based on atmospheric fixation of nitrogen, which at one stroke solved a major problem of agricultural production.

On the theoretical side, the knowledge of molecular structure developed in physics was being used in chemistry, while physics was beginning to explore nuclear and electronic phenomena within the atom; and this in turn was to provide extraordinary new insights into the nature of chemical processes.

These were the new frontiers that beckoned young men like Hendricks into chemistry. I have heard him exclaim many times that he has been fortunate to live in the Golden Age of science, which makes our era the most wonderful in history. A scientist's credo.

Cottrell had succeeded in helping to establish a United

States nitrate industry and was reorienting his laboratory toward some basic research. (The laboratory disappeared in 1939 with the reorganization of the scientific work of the Department of Agriculture under the new Agricultural Research Administration, when soils investigation was transferred to the Bureau of Plant Industry.) He welcomed young Hendricks and characteristically told him to do whatever he wanted. This set a pattern, and Hendricks had a free hand thereafter. For those with the self-discipline and self-direction needed to make the best use of such freedom, it is the *sine qua non*—as creative artists know—for the effective fusion of imagination and knowledge. Basic research, I think, is this fusion.

Instruments have had a profound influence on scientific discovery. Without instruments, the brilliant reasoning and keen observation of the Greeks could take them only so far in investigating the nature of the physical universe. Leeuwenhoek's crude little magnifier revealed a hitherto invisible world of life that explained a large number of phenomena that could be controlled only when they were understood.

Hendricks' research has been based largely on the X-ray spectroscope and similar instruments designed for sleuthing in the realm of molecules and atoms and studying the fine structure of matter, particularly crystals. At the time he joined the Department of Agriculture, he was one of the very few experts in the use of the new technique.

When visible light is passed through a lattice or grating of parallel lines the same distance apart as the length of the light wave, it is diffracted, or broken up, into a pattern of alternating light and dark bands. The same thing occurs with the invisible X-rays at the far end of the spectrum. Since X-rays have extremely short wave lengths, the lattice has to be correspondingly fine. These short waves can penetrate most solids because they slip into the interstices between molecules or atoms. In a crystal, molecules and atoms are arranged in a regular pattern, which can be determined by the use of the X-ray lattice and recorded photographically as dots or bands, or observed in other ways. This, plus the use of collateral data and mathematical formulas, is essentially the X-ray diffraction technique. It can provide information about the pattern and size of the crystalline cell, the number of molecules in the cell, the symmetry of the individual molecules, the position of the atoms in the molecules (most important of all), and the distances between the atoms.

Thus the X-ray spectroscope is a powerful research tool. Hendricks was the only person in the United States government who had one and knew how to use it. There were only a hundred in the world, most of them owned by private industry. With it, and later with similar instruments, he was able to do a great deal of original spadework.

Hendricks has, of course, done a good many things in thirty-five years of research, but his principal contributions have been in four main areas.

(1) He was the first to discover the true nature of clays as crystalline rather than jellylike (colloidal) material. Men can live on earth because plants can grow here. Plants can grow because the earth has a thin layer of soil covering a mass of other material; for comparison, the soil is equivalent in thickness to a sheet of tissue paper pasted on a sphere seven feet in diameter. The soil is fertile

because it contains clay, which stores and releases chemical nutrients to feed plants. The work of Hendricks resulted in a far more accurate understanding of how and why clays do these things (and others) than had been possible before.

(2) Hendricks (with his co-workers) was the first to develop a sure-fire method for finding out where a peculiarly flexible and adaptable force known chemically as the "hydrogen bond" is operating in chemical substances, and for measuring its effects quantitatively. This discovery has been a major factor in stimulating a vast increase in hydrogen-bond studies, which in turn are showing that this force is one of the most universal in nature and a key to some of the deepest secrets of life—for example, the structure of genes, which exist in the nucleus of every cell in a plant or animal and are the means of transmitting inheritance.

(3) In studying the mineral nutrition of plants, Hendricks and his co-workers discovered how roots get nourishment from the soil—how living cells pull a needed chemical from a weak solution outside the cell wall to the strong solution inside the cell. The phenomenon has never been understood, yet it is an essential part of a wide range of life processes in both plants and animals. The first work, done with phosphorus, is being extended to other mineral nutrients and will help to solve some difficult physiological problems.

(4) One of the most striking phenomena in nature is the decisive influence of the alternating day-night or light-dark rhythm on the life processes of plants, including growth, flowering, and seed germination. This was first

discovered in the Department of Agriculture in 1918 and has had wide practical application. The how and why of the phenomenon remained a complete mystery until Hendricks and Borthwick and their co-workers discovered in 1962 that the whole range of complex processes is controlled by tiny specks of a blue chemical in specific parts of the plant; and the chemical, in turn, is activated by red light of specific wave lengths. This chemical, hitherto unknown, is as important to plants as the pituitary hormones are to human beings.

The first subject Hendricks turned to was the study of clay. His associates in this work were C. S. Ross, of the United States Geological Survey, and L. T. Alexander, of Agriculture's United States Soil Survey.

Clay is the chemically dynamic constituent of soils. It not only stores and releases plant nutrients but, in combination with organic matter, it determines soil structure, which in turn determines tilth, or cultivability. Its importance to mankind agriculturally and otherwise is beyond calculation. Empirically, clays were rather well understood; for centuries before modern times man had been growing crops in them, and had been using clays to make houses, cooking pots, and water jugs. Scientifically, though, clays were misunderstood, since they were generally considered to be of jellylike (colloidal) material.

When Hendricks examined clay with his powerful new research instrument, he immediately obtained the diffraction patterns characteristic of crystals. Clay, he saw, is not amorphous; it consists of an infinite number of minute mineral crystals geometrically as regular as diamonds or snowflakes. Thus chemically and physically it must behave like crystals, not like colloids.

This was contrary to the prevailing and official view. Viewpoints, like wagon wheels, tend to stay in the ruts they themselves have made. It is an understatement to say that Hendricks was not officially encouraged in Agriculture to continue with this unorthodox inquiry; but having practiced swimming rapids feet first so his head would not hit the rocks, he continued nevertheless. The Geological Survey gave him enthusiastic support and rounded up a world-wide collection of clay samples for X-ray scrutiny.

Hendricks examined them systematically. He found that there are some twenty-five principal kinds of clay, and over a period of about fifteen years he determined the chemical composition and detailed structure of all of them, as well as their behavior in soils. The atoms are chiefly silicon, aluminum, and oxygen, with small amounts of hydrogen and some other minerals such as calcium, magnesium, sodium, and potassium. The silicate (silicon-oxygen) atoms form tetrahedrons linked together in sheets that readily split into exceedingly thin layers, which build up like a pile of typewriter paper and are held together by aluminum atoms. (All this is submicroscopic, of course.)

At the surfaces of the sheets, which are perhaps six or eight atoms thick, there are chiefly oxygen or hydroxyl atoms. (Hydroxyl is an oxygen and a hydrogen atom so combined that they behave as one unit.) Clays with predominantly oxygen surfaces attract water; in other words, they get wet, like a pane of glass in the rain. If glass were wax, it would not get wet. The wettable clays collect so much water between (not inside) the sheets that they swell; they are called swelling clays. The swelling clays are the important ones agriculturally because they do hold water, and the water, in turn, contains dissolved plant nutrients. Indonesia can feed enormous numbers of people because its soils are rich in a swelling clay from local volcanoes. India has much more difficulty feeding a large population: its soils are generally poor in these clays.

The whole process—of holding water and absorbing its plant nutrients—is a matter of *surface* chemistry, and the surface areas involved are enormous because clay is so finely divided by progressive splitting into thinner and thinner sheets. It has been calculated that if the surfaces of all of the particles in two ounces of clay—one generous jigger—could be spread out they would cover an acre of land, or 43,560 square feet. How many jiggers of clay are there in an acre? Enough, perhaps, to cover the earth if the particle surfaces could be spread out.

This is how plants manage to thrive in a difficult world; the clay particles are a vast storehouse of nutrients. The whole complex is an admirable, intricate arrangement for supporting life, with the parts fitting together like a sub-microscopic jigsaw puzzle—one that Hendricks notably helped to solve.

There were many other interesting aspects of this work with clays; and while it is primarily useful to agricultural scientists, providing a solid foundation for subsequent applied research and practice, it has also been useful in major areas other than agriculture. Clays are extremely important in the petroleum industry, for example, first for the so-called muds used in drilling, and later in the catalytic cracking process that produces gasoline through chemical reactions on the surfaces of clay particles. Millions of dollars can be wasted, for example, if you use the wrong kind of clay. About once a year efforts were made to lure Hendricks out of agriculture into oil. (He was also approached to serve as head of metallurgy at Los Alamos during the atom bomb days because of his knowledge of the structure of metals.) Basic facts developed in Hendricks' research are of importance likewise in road building, where the subsurface is clay and the surface is claylike cement (swelling clays in the subsurface can cause serious buckling, as they did in Mexico City); and in the ceramics and brick industries, where clay is the raw material.

Hendricks has done very little work in crystal structure for a good many years. The field has become enormously complicated. There are so many atoms in a complex molecule that to get the whole diffraction pattern you have to handle equations containing thousands of terms, which you feed into mechanical computers. Hendricks prefers to spend his time otherwise.

At do-it-yourself computing, however, he is expert. In the clay work he used matrix algebra to determine what would be the probable order of succession of random layers of silicates and water, and also the probable effects of irregularities in crystals caused by the breaking of atoms when clay layers split apart, as they do constantly in nature. Broken or irregular crystals have very different properties, in some respects, from regular crystals of the same substance; and often these properties prove to be extremely useful. Hendricks worked out the irregular structure of the ferromagnetic form of iron oxide; later the oxide was used for the sound-sensitive coating of all recording tapes, an application that he, the basic researcher, could not foresee but that the applied researcher could. Transistors are another example of flawed crystals with valuable properties.

Matrix algebra is a neat mathematical method of calculating the probable result of interaction among an infinite number of units—electrons, for example—all behaving more or less independently. In the submicroscopic world, where it is not possible to predict what will happen to any one unit, the probable aggregate effect of all the forces is the substitute for certainty. Mechanical computers operate on the principles of matrix algebra.

Early in the 1930's, while he was still occupied with molecular structure, Hendricks started another major line of research in the same general field. This became a five-year investigation of the hydrogen bond, or H bond, the cementing force that makes possible the infinitely complex architecture of the human body.

Atoms are usually held together in molecules by chemical bonds so strong that they cannot be broken, to permit the atoms to recombine in new substances, without the use of considerable energy. In some substances, however, the bonds are much weaker—so much weaker that the aggregates of atoms are not even called molecules but "complexes," and the atoms are said to be held together by "association." Such a complex is not only readily formed; it can be readily broken and reversed, to return to the original state. The force most commonly responsible for these complexes is the hydrogen bond.

Hydrogen is the most common of the elements. Water, the most common of earthly compounds, is an H-bonded association of hydrogen and hydroxyl atoms. It is a part of all organic substances. "All living things evolved from and exist in an aqueous solution," and life as we know it on our planet would not be possible without water. It is the H-bond that gives water its extraordinary ability to dissolve substances, hold them in solution, and combine them. Because of this ability, water, with its hydrogen bond, plays a key part in practically everything we eat and wear and use. And everything we do; for at the atomic level the H-bond makes possible the subtle, continuous, reversible chemical changes involved in muscular activity, nerve functioning (probably including memory), endocrine activity, and the genetic structure that underlies inheritance and development. "Man himself is fabricated of hydrogen-bonded substances."

This understanding of the fundamental nature and widespread influence of the H-bond is new and in many ways still on the frontiers of research. As in the case of clays, Hendricks had a pioneering role in making the development of this new knowledge possible. Incidentally, the H-bond is a prime factor in the usefulness of agricultural clays, through their combination with water.

The instrument for the H-bond studies was likewise a spectroscope, but this time one that used infrared light— the long light waves at the opposite end of the spectrum from X-rays. This spectroscope was a homemade affair built by F. S. Brackett at a cost of some $1,000. (Hendricks has a store-bought one in his laboratory today. It cost about $30,000. But nowadays the instruments are electronic and much more elaborate.) His co-workers on the H-bond team were G. E. Gilbert (organic chemistry), O. R. Wulf (molecular physics), and Urner Liddell (physics), who operated the spectroscope.

When Hendricks exposed material containing the hydroxyl group to infrared radiation, he found that in certain areas the material did not absorb the radiation as it did everywhere else. The failure to absorb infrared radiation coincided in all cases with the presence of a hydrogen bond. It was a definitive test.

(Hendricks' spectroscopes remind me of the stuff Alice took to smallen herself so she could get down the rabbit hole and open the door to a fascinating wonderland for everyone who reads the book. His career has been essentially one of opening doors through which others might pass to farther reaches of knowledge.)

H-bond and *H-bomb* sound almost the same phonetically, Hendricks remarks, but conceptually they are poles apart. The *H-bond* is as mild and unobtrusive as a drop of water, yet one of the most positive creative forces in nature, and so universally distributed that the number of bonds existing at any given moment is too immense even to be guessed. The *H-bomb,* as lurid as its mushroom cloud, is the most negative, destroying force at man's disposal, but fortunately rare.

(*Rare* in this case, if one may pun,
Is overdone.)

✱

In 1963, Hendricks' current research was in two fields, both very broad and fundamental.

One was the mineral nutrition of plants. The aspect he was investigating may be summed up in the question: How does a plant root take up mineral nutrients from the soil? In thousands of years of agriculture, no one has answered this question or even proposed a satisfactory answer.

Why is the question difficult to answer? Because the mineral, or mineral salt—phosphate, potash, or whatever it may be—has to pass through a membrane, the cell wall of the root, and the concentration of the mineral in the plant juice inside the cell is considerably greater than in the soil solution outside. If the situation were reversed so that the plant solution became more dilute rather than more concentrated, there would be no problem; the phenomenon would be the familiar one of osmosis, in which water moves through a membrane from a less to a more concentrated solution until the concentration is equal on both sides. For the mineral to move the other way, however, is like pushing an object uphill, compared with letting it roll down. It takes energy.

Where does the energy come from? What runs this biological pumping system? The problem is as baffling in the animal as in the plant kingdom. Similar transfers across membranes occur constantly in the stomach, kidneys, and red blood cells of the human body.

The answer or answers would enlarge our understanding of many important biological processes. The problem is one of comparative biochemistry, and whatever clues are found in one field will at once be useful in the other.

Hendricks and his co-workers, the late Cal Hagen, Everett Leggett, and Patricia Jackson, started with phosphate. Among the functions of phosphorus in plant and animal organisms, two are outstanding: it combines with other elements to produce compounds that have great value as sources of energy, and it plays a part in the structure of nucleic acids, the material of which genes are made. Hendricks began with phosphorus because he had been working on phosphate fertilizers with the new radioactive-tracer technique that was a by-product of wartime atomic research. Most chemical elements have isotopes, or alternate forms that are identical in every way with the original element except that they are radioactive. An atom of an isotope that is radioactive can be traced through all its travels and transformations in an organism by means of Geiger counters and other devices to detect the radiation. During the past few years much practical information about fertilizer use—where, when, how, how much—has been developed from studies with isotopes provided by the Atomic Energy Commission.

The tracer technique disclosed the nature of the energy that pumps phosphorus from the weak solution in the soil through the cell wall into the strong solution inside the plant. The complex process might be summarized like this:

As the root of the plant breathes, it draws oxygen from the soil. The oxygen combines with sugar in the root, and the chemical reaction gives off energy. This is the force that pumps phosphorus into the plant. Once inside, the phosphorus forms a new compound that the plant stores. Like sugar, phosphorus is a rich source of energy—as it is also in human muscle; a man is like a cabbage in more ways than he realizes.

Under intensive study next was potassium. One of its major functions in both plants and animals is to reduce acidity to the levels best for the organism. The problem here, too, is one of transfer from a weak to a more concentrated solution; the soil contains very little potash, and the plant a great deal. (It was called *potash*—whence *potassium*—because it is the ash left in the pot when plant material is burned.) An analogous situation occurs in nerve and muscle fibers. Whatever the final answer, it will be quite different, Hendricks says, from the phosphorus mechanism.

In accordance with good laboratory principles, the experiments were simplified as much as possible. One way was to cut the roots off and work with them alone instead of with the whole plant, since they continue to live and function. From a big jar of water Hendricks pulled a mass of pale, wet, stringy stuff to show me. It looked like a platinum-blond mermaid's hair. Shorn barley roots, he said.

The second major area of Hendricks' recent research has been concerned with the rhythmic succession of light and dark, day and night, that governs the major biological functioning of all plants except the lowest orders. The light-dark rhythm governs the germination of seed, vegetative growth of stem and leaf, flowering (sex and reproduction), the onset of winter dormancy, the autumnal coloring of foliage, the autumnal abscission or falling of leaves, the onset of renewed vernal activity, and various other manifestations of the vitality of plants—the reddening of apples, for example.

A minute quantity of a protein substance joined to a bright blue pigment and located in the leaves triggers all of these activities. The amount in each plant—or each embryo in the seed—is perhaps 1/10,000 of 1 percent of the weight of the organism.

The pigment is sensitive to light, especially to the long waves at the red end of the spectrum. Like Dr. Jekyll and Mr. Hyde, it alternately assumes two forms (except that neither is morally evil)—Dr. Jekyll in daylight, Mr. Hyde at night. Dr. Jekyll, the daylight and active form, we might designate as Pigment 735, or P735, because it absorbs light waves about 735 millimicrons in length at the far-red end of the spectrum, adjacent to and overlapping infrared. (A millimicron is 1/10,000 of a millimeter, or about four millionths of an inch.) Mr. Hyde, the nocturnal and negative form, is nothing more than inactivated or inverted P735. We might designate it P660, since it absorbs light waves about 660 millimicrons in length, to the left of far-red.

The active, daylight P735 is the form that initiates flower development, which in turn inhibits further stem growth. The inactivated, nocturnal P660 does not induce development but does permit vegetative growth. In nature, the light at dawn, about half an hour before sunrise, starts the formation of P735. It is active throughout the daylight hours and for about two hours after dark. Then it reverts—the chemical term is "isomerizes"—to P660, which in turn becomes P735 at dawn.

In nature, weed seed buried in the ground will not germinate until it has been exposed to light, as by plowing. Seed has stayed dormant eighty years (authenticated—possibly 300 years, unauthenticated) and then germinated on exposure. (As a result of this discovery, the trend now is to reduce plowing to a minimum as a method of weed control.) Seed of agricultural crops, of course, is exposed to light in the process of handling and planting. Laboratory tests show that germination, like flowering, is triggered by P735 and inhibited by P660. Germination has been started and stopped and started and stopped many times in the same seed by alternating exposure to the two wave lengths so that the pigments shuttled back and forth, as it were, from one form to the other. Similarly, flowering has been alternately started and suppressed; and small plants only a few days old have been stimulated to precocious sexual development (flowering) by exposure to far-red.

In fact, laboratory studies of an extraordinary variety and precision have been (and are being) carried out to pinpoint the multiform influence of the blue pigment, which has been named "phytochrome" by its discoverers, one of whom is Hendricks.

Phytochrome is as important in human affairs as chlorophyll, the green coloring matter of leaves. Using the energy of sunlight, chlorophyll is the originator of all our food and many other necessities, including wood, cloth, paper, coal, and gasoline. And phytochrome, through its control of growth and reproduction, controls the formation of chlorophyll. Phytochrome might be likened to a master electric switch turned on and off by variations in light, or to the pituitary hormone that has such extensive authority in our bodies.

The discoverers of phytochrome knew about its existence and general character from spectroscopic evidence
before they saw it. The instrument used was a spectro-
photometer—a device that measures the intensity of light
passing through various substances. This one had been
especially modified by two Department of Agriculture
marketing experts, Karl Norris and Warren Butler, for
examining fruit to detect internal decay. They worked
with H. A. Borthwick, H. W. Siegelman, and Hendricks
on the phytochrome investigations, as did Eben and Vivian
Toole, U.S.D.A. seed experts. In 1962 the group succeeded
in isolating and collecting about as much phytochrome as
would cover the head of a pin without spilling over, but
enough for preliminary analysis to determine its chemical
nature. (The isolation has not yet been officially reported
as this is written, in April, 1963.) They expected to collect
a great deal more for thorough study, using a huge ton-
nage of corn seedlings to accumulate it.

The research on phytochrome originated with the work
of the late W. W. Garner and H. T. Allard, the two Agriculture Department plant breeders who first reported in
1918 that "the relative length of day and night" was the
factor determining when the terminal shoot of a tobacco
and a soybean plant would stop growing and produce a
blossom. They soon found that there are "short-day" plants
like soybeans and corn, "long-day" plants like wheat and
barley, and plants that are apparently not affected by day
length (though in fact light-responsive).

This response—"photoperiodism," they called it—was
a startling discovery that soon had practical applications.
For example, varieties of soybeans, a major crop, are bred

to suit the specific average growing-season day length in each 200-mile-wide area from south to north. (In nature it is the *average* seasonal daily light-dark ratio that governs plant reactions, not the one-shot treatment given under laboratory conditions.) Florists and nurserymen, whose products have a high economic value (the rose is almost as important as the potato economically), make extensive use of controlled light. Chrysanthemums, an autumnal short-day plant, can be brought to bloom at any time for the florist trade by the use of shade or light to control day length. Current experiments have increased growth tenfold, as a result of lengthening the day with artificial light. This is a finding that may have considerable value in forestry, not only to speed growth but to hasten maturity of trees so as to produce hybrid seed in less time than would be possible under natural conditions.

Following Garner and Allard, the research on photoperiodism was taken over by H. A. Borthwick and M. W. Parker early in 1936. In 1944 Hendricks joined them, and the subsequent research was carried on by this team and their co-workers until Parker left the group in 1952, to be appointed later as head of crops work in the Department of Agriculture.

This brief account touches only high lights, omitting the supporting evidence and the rich details that keep turning up like diamonds in the blue ground of Kimberley. The findings have been more far-reaching than anyone could have dreamed when the phenomenon of photoperiodism was first noted.

We already know a good deal about phytochrome, Hendricks says, but it may take five years to confirm what is now still hypothesis and to work out details. We know that phytochrome is a specific kind of pyrolle. Pyrolles are building blocks of some pigments with unusual properties, including chlorophyll and heme, the red pigment in hemoglobin that transports oxygen in our blood. This particular pyrolle is a phycocyanin, the coloring material of blue-green algae. Chemically it is related to bile acids in the human body. We know phytochrome behaves like a hormone. Since it does not move out of the leaf, we know that it must somehow send a message to the point where growth and flowering occur.

What is the messenger, and how does it convey the message? Hendricks thinks it may be a co-enzyme. Co-enzymes are chemical messengers in biological systems. A co-enzyme delivers the catalytic stimulus of an enzyme to the point where the reaction is to take place, and does it over and over again. Hendricks believes that, like an enzyme, phytochrome catalyzes, or initiates, one specific reaction, and only one, in the plant. All the diverse phenomena of flowering, germination, and so on are manifestations of that one reaction—just as the main switch in a house controls lights, furnace, refrigerator, water heater, and air conditioner but really does only one thing: closes a gap so that electric current can flow through a circuit.

As Hendricks points out, the diurnal alternation of light and dark and its seasonal variation is the clock that regulates many biological responses in animals as well as plants. It notifies the purple martin in Maryland, U.S.A., or elsewhere that the time has come to take off for Brazil, and vice versa. Before the snow comes, it tells the snow rabbit to change to his white coat so he will not be conspicuous. It notifies the salmon when to head back to its native river for the spawning season. In human beings the biological rhythm is often concealed or distorted, but it is present nonetheless, as in ovulation and in cell division in the skin. This division occurs at two o'clock each morning and only then—a fact discovered accidentally from examination of circumcised foreskins in a hospital.

The plant and animal researchers in this field watch one another's work with keen interest.

Hendricks' major contributions have been in the four areas of clay structure, the H-bond, mineral nutrition, and phytochrome. All four are interconnected in many ways, and his interest in them grew out of his early training in physical chemistry. In the selection both of a career and of subsequent fields of activity within it, however, he gives a good deal of weight to sheer accident. He considers that the most important condition for successful research is freedom to choose what to do and how to do it. It is this that gives the work endless zest.

He has made many other contributions besides these. The work on crystal structure, for example, led to new knowledge of compounds such as iron carbide, which is responsible for the hardness of iron. Work on phosphate fertilizers involved study of the crystal structure of phosphate rock, which in turn led to Hendricks' discovery that bone, which is a similar material, has exactly the same crystal structure and that the crystals grow in the same way —a problem medicine had been trying to solve for 200 years. (Incidentally, the finding explains how fluoride, which is present in phosphate rock, enters into tooth formation to prevent decay.) His determination of the method by which crystals take up heat—molecular rotation—attracted considerable scientific attention. He developed detailed information, not hitherto available, about the behavior of electrically charged particles (cations) responsible for the binding and releasing of nutrients by the soil. He contributed to establishing a metric for organic compounds—that is, an exact measurement of the distances between atoms in crystals. He worked out the method by which rubber latex is formed in plants, and this led to a better general concept of plant biosynthesis.

Throughout, I think the outstanding Hendricks' trait is the refusal to be pigeonholed, confined to some narrow crevasse of specialization. Hendricks prefers the view from a mountain and enjoys the hard climb up to it. He tends to think of scientific knowledge as a unity; the important thing is to develop the interrelation, not the fragmentation, of the parts. His range of interest and information is correspondingly broad.

I think Byron Shaw, who directs the scientific research of the Department of Agriculture, had in mind Hendricks' general approach and procedure, and its outstanding effectiveness, when he developed the Agriculture Department's pioneering research laboratories. Hendricks' work was an example of what Shaw wanted to accomplish. It showed that in agriculture, as well as in such fields as the cracking of the atom, the long, steady drive on basic research objectives can pay off in fundamental knowledge that will be useful to scores or hundreds of scientists seeking to develop new and better products and practices. The first laboratory, established in August, 1957, was the one at Beltsville, Maryland, concerned with the mineral nutrition of plants, with Hendricks as leader; this is where the phosphorus and potassium work was done. Two months later Shaw established the Plant Physiology Laboratory at Beltsville, with Borthwick as leader and Hendricks as an informal associate; this is the home of the phytochrome work.

Early in 1963 there were twenty of these pioneering laboratories in various parts of the United States, each involved in some field of basic research peculiarly significant to agriculture yet with much wider ramifications; each led by a scientist who had shown outstanding ability to do independent original work in that field; each so free of bureaucratic atmosphere that no one is called head or director or has to waste time administering when he might be working.

Back of this is an even more fundamental step. With the support of the Civil Service Commission, Shaw succeeded in breaking the old and vicious division between scientific research and administration in Agriculture (and subsequently this was done in other agencies). Formerly, no research scientist could reach as high a level of grade or salary as an administrator could. If he wanted or needed to go higher he had to give up research and become an administrator—or go elsewhere to work. No one knows how much this situation has meant to the government in loss of top scientific talent, through failure to attract or retain the best men available. Shaw succeeded in equating the grades and salaries of scientists and administrators so that today an able man can stay in research, if that is his choice, without handicapping himself and his family financially. Hendricks, working with a few people in two small laboratories, reached the same grade and received the same salary as Shaw, who administered all the far-flung research of the Department.

The credit is not by any means all Shaw's and Hendricks'. For one thing, both men came along at a time when research gets special attention and also has special urgency for the sake of the nation's future. They contributed scientific statesmanship to meet the nation's need.

Colin F. Stam

A STUDY IN ANONYMOUS POWER

E. W. KENWORTHY

THE TRUSTEES OF
PRINCETON UNIVERSITY

BY VIRTUE OF THE AUTHORITY VESTED IN THEM

UNDER A PROGRAM INITIATED BY JOHN D. ROCKEFELLER 3RD

TO STRENGTHEN THE CAREER

SERVICE IN THE FEDERAL GOVERNMENT

DO HEREBY GRANT A

ROCKEFELLER PUBLIC SERVICE AWARD

TO

COLIN F. STAM

IN RECOGNITION OF DISTINGUISHED SERVICE

TO THE GOVERNMENT OF THE UNITED STATES

AND TO THE AMERICAN PEOPLE

PRESIDENT

CLERK

DONE IN NASSAU HALL
PRINCETON, NEW JERSEY

COLIN F. STAM

Most evenings, when the weather is fine, an elderly, somewhat corpulent man may be seen walking a lugubrious basset hound near Chevy Chase Circle in northwest Washington.

His round, abstracted face is surmounted by a scrunched-up felt hat. His collar is rumpled and his tie askew. Even on warm evenings he is likely to wear a sweater under his jacket, below which a trim of shirttail often shows. Passers-by old enough to remember Scattergood Baines may smile as if they had suddenly come upon that character of Clarence Budington Kelland.

The stroller is Colin Ferguson Stam and he is Chief of Staff of the Joint Congressional Committee on Internal Revenue Taxation. To most of those who for years have seen him taking the air with his dog—it used to be a chow —or buying a chocolate bar at the local drugstore, he is as unknown as he is to virtually all of the other 42,531,000 Americans who in 1962 struggled with Form 1040.

But Colin Stam is not entirely unknown or without fame. In recognition of his reputation in the mysteries of taxation, Dartmouth College bestowed upon him in 1958 an honorary degree of doctor of laws. And Princeton picked him in 1961 for the coveted Rockefeller Public Service Award.

To attorneys in the great law firms who make their living out of "the continuing struggle among contending interests for the privilege of paying the least," Stam is an office word synonymous with the Internal Revenue Code. On Capitol Hill, in the House Ways and Means Committee and the Senate Finance Committee, in the Treasury and its Internal Revenue Service, his name is one to conjure with. And among reporters in the House and Senate press galleries he is known as the man who knows all about a pending tax bill, and tells nothing.

Submerged in the vast bureaucracy of Washington are a number of civil servants whose great but anonymous influence on public affairs is known only to their headlined superiors, to experts in their field, and to the press. But the power and influence of none of these faceless men approaches that wielded by Stam over the past twenty-five years.

One lawyer who has been in both government and private practice swears that on tax legislation Stam has had more influence than the President, the Secretary of the Treasury, the assistant secretary in charge of taxation, the chairmen of the tax-writing committees in Congress—separately or combined.

Stam would deny this, and admittedly it is a slight exaggeration. Another lawyer puts it more soberly: "Stam is the most omnipotent but anonymous civil servant in the government." And a third says: "No other man's hand is as conspicuous on the pages of tax legislation as this man's."

To state this power in cautionary terms, only one out of twenty authorities interviewed by this writer was willing to have his views of Stam attributed to him. He was Senator Harry F. Byrd, Chairman of the Finance Committee, who has always relied closely on Stam for advice on tax matters. The rest said without apology that Stam's power in this sensitive area was so great that they could not risk quotation by name.

Anyone seeking information on Stam will search in vain for his name in standard works on taxation and articles in the law school journals, although references abound to the "Chief of Staff" of the Joint Committee and "his profound influence over tax policy decisions." He has written occasionally for professional journals, and there are sparse, and usually perfunctory, references to him in newspaper morgues.

How did this civil servant, who has served nine different chairmen of the tax committees under six administrations, achieve such power? How has he exercised it? What manner of man is he? What is the net effect of his stewardship?

Colin Ferguson Stam was born August 27, 1896, in Chestertown on the Eastern Shore of Maryland. His mother's people were English stock, his father's Dutch. In its customs and attitudes, Chestertown was Southern and conservative. There Stam grew up, and attended public school and Washington College, from which he received his B.A. degree in 1916.

After service as a Navy ensign in World War I, he came to Washington and got a bottom-rung job in the Internal Revenue Bureau, which enabled him to pay for night classes at Georgetown University Law School. In 1922 he took his LL.B., passed his bar examinations, and became an attorney in the Internal Revenue Bureau, where he worked in the Division of Rules and Regulations interpreting the statutes.

In 1923 and 1924 Stam took special courses in taxation at George Washington University Law School. In 1926 he was transferred to the Office of General Counsel of the Internal Revenue Bureau. His stay there was short. The Treasury had detailed him to prepare data for a report that Congress had ordered from the newly created Joint Committee on Internal Revenue Taxation. His work came to the attention of the committee's counsel, who invited Stam to be his assistant in 1927. Stam accepted. The rest of his life has been largely the history of federal tax legislation.

The mental stimulus and exaltation of spirit that some men experience in the contemplation of first principles, others find in "the nice sharp squillets of the law," such as—dipping at random into the Internal Revenue Code:

"For purposes of subsection (b), the term 'regulated public utility' does not (except as provided in paragraph [3]) include a corporation described in paragraph (1) unless 80 per cent or more of its gross income (computed without regard to dividends and capital gains and losses) for the taxable year is derived from sources described in paragraph (1)."

Such a man is Colin Stam.

There are men also who care very little about public recognition or display of power, or its perquisites, but very much for the reality of power in the recesses where policy decisions are made.

Such a man, also, is Stam.

He had not determined on a career in tax legislation when he went to law school. How happy an accident, then, that his first job was in the Internal Revenue Bureau, and even more fortuitous the invitation to be assistant counsel of the Joint Committee. For in tax law he would find a field congenial to his talents and disposition. And in the scrubby labors of the Joint Committee staff, he would discover unsuspected power opportunities.

The Joint Committee on Internal Revenue Taxation, the first such committee to be set up by Congress, was created by statute in 1926. It was composed of ten members, five each from the House Ways and Means and Senate Finance committees, with each group represented by three from the majority party and two from the minority, and with the understanding that the chairmen and ranking members of each would serve.

The Joint Committee was an outgrowth of the investigation of the Internal Revenue Bureau in 1924-25 by Senator James Couzens of Michigan. Indeed, it had been set up in an effort to sidetrack further investigation by that progressive Republican, who had raised a considerable stir over the operations of the Internal Revenue Bureau, and particularly its handling of large refunds. As a result there had been agitation for the establishment of an independent commission to keep an eye on administration of the tax laws.

In order to quiet this agitation and still keep the investigation under congressional surveillance and control, the leadership hit on the idea of a joint committee. In the statute creating the committee, Congress directed it to prepare a report by the end of 1927, with recommendations on various proposals for changing and simplifying the tax laws.

Obviously the Joint Committee needed expert help, and a staff of lawyers, accountants, and statisticians was engaged. The committee was expected to go out of business when it completed its report in the following Congress.

This was not to be, and the reasons why Congress made it a standing committee with a permanent staff are obvious enough. The original income tax law of 1913 was simplicity itself. Congress set up an exemption of $3,000, was lenient on the middle brackets, established a maximum surtax of 6 per cent on incomes over $500,000, and did not foresee a time when anything more confiscatory would be justified. Complexity began with the excess-profits tax of World War I, but Congress viewed this as an expedient to be ended after the war. The skein had been started, however, and through the Twenties it became increasingly tangled.

To deal with this complexity, the Treasury had its experts, and industry its lawyers. But the House Ways and

Means and Senate Finance committees had nobody. Their staffs were small, composed of nonprofessional appointees who came and went with shifts in political power.

The tax committees were fully aware of their constitutional prerogatives and jealous to preserve them, for they knew that political nerve ends, especially of influential groups and constituents, are most sensitive to the tax touch. Instinctively they suspected the Executive's tax proposals and supporting data, but increasingly the members found themselves technically unequipped to do battle. The Treasury would come up to Capitol Hill with a plan, and there was no one to meet the enemy at the gate. Little wonder, then, that the chairmen and committee members welcomed the idea of an expert staff that would be fore-armed with independent studies and an intimate knowledge of their attitudes and predispositions.

And so the Joint Committee—which for all practical purposes meant its staff—was assigned the duties of investigating and making recommendations on (1) the operation and effects of the internal revenue laws, (2) their administration by the Internal Revenue Bureau (now the Internal Revenue Service), and (3) their simplification. In addition, the Joint Committee—and this again meant the staff—was required to approve all refunds over $100,-000 before they were made.

It should be noted that there is nothing in the statute that empowers the staff or its chief to assist in the actual preparation of tax legislation. It says much, therefore, for the competence of the staff from the outset and for the confidence placed in it that by 1930, four years after its formation, the Joint Committee formally directed its staff to work on legislation. This authority it has enjoyed ever since, not by law but by practice.

In 1929 Stam became the Joint Committee's counsel and began a labor that would have daunted a less painstaking man. This was the codifying of the internal revenue laws. The last codification had been in 1873. Since then the miscellaneous acts had become an impenetrable thicket full of exceptions, inconsistencies, and overlappings. Stam set out to reduce this disorder to a body of statutory law: rephrasing, consolidating, and simplifying without modifying the intent of Congress. At the outset the Treasury and many tax lawyers were dubious about this venturesome undertaking. As one lawyer who participated in the work said: "Treasury was afraid to let anybody try to put that ocean into a pint pot."

It took ten years to complete the task. When it was finished, the Treasury, the Congress, the legal fraternity, and the Bench agreed that the Internal Revenue Code of 1939 was a triumph of exacting scholarship. But Stam's worth had already been recognized by the Joint Committee, which had made him Chief of Staff the year before.

It was the view of Mr. Justice Holmes that citizens ought not look on taxes as a wicked imposition but rather regard them as a political tithe to be cheerfully borne, since they are "what we pay for civilized society."

This is a generous, manly sentiment to which many taxpayers might subscribe—as an abstract proposition. But as the distinguished tax lawyer, Louis Eisenstein, writes in his *Ideologies of Taxation,* a witty and decanted discourse on a cloudy subject, there are some practical difficulties with Mr. Justice Holmes's definition. First, not every taxpayer, individual or corporative, is necessarily "happy to bear his allotted share." Second, many taxpayers seriously question whether the shares have been allotted fairly, and whether they are not paying for a larger portion of civilization than they receive. Finally, there are groups who are firmly convinced that, since their functions are so "peculiarly vital to the progress of civilization" and their contributions so exceptional, their taxes should be correspondingly small.

From the resulting clashes of interest brought to bear on the Treasury's proposals, emerges a tax bill.

Stam would readily acknowledge that he has been intimately involved in this resolution of forces for a quarter century—but only as a supplier of data, analyses, and, when solicited, counsel. He disclaims any role as a policy maker. Policy making, he maintains, is a right that belongs only to the elected members of the tax committees.

In an ultimate sense, this is true, because the House Ways and Means and Senate Finance committees can, of course, reject the counsel they have sought—and sometimes do. Nevertheless, Senator Harry F. Byrd was again the only one discovered by this writer to agree with Stam's modest evaluation of his role. After stating that "Stam doesn't control tax policies, he gives his opinion frankly," Byrd went on to say: "He has made very many vital decisions. He has made recommendations that have carried great weight with both committees."

More representative of the views of most experts in the field is that expressed by Stanley S. Surrey, former Harvard professor, appointed Assistant Secretary of the Treasury for tax matters in 1961. In the *Harvard Law Review* for May, 1957, he wrote:

"The members of this staff work closely with the Treasury technicians. Their work on the details of proposals and drafts is highly important, but the task of policy formulation and policy guidance to the congressmen appears to be reserved exclusively to the chief of staff."

Whence derives this influence? Chiefly from three things:

First, there is Stam's profound knowledge of the law. A former Treasury expert who doubts whether, on the whole, Stam's influence on tax policy has been salutary, says:

"He knows more about the background of every sentence in the revenue code and the reason it was written the way it was, the technical problems it sought to deal with, and the problems it has raised, than any other mortal. This is the source of his strength."

Because of this knowledge, members of the tax-writing committees feel they are not at the mercy of Treasury experts and know they can find reinforcement for their opposition to proposals they dislike or suspect, either instinctively or on the urging of influential interests and constituents.

Second, there is Stam's ability, because of his knowledge, to keep the committees out of trouble, and individual members from making fools of themselves, by pressing unwise or indefensible amendments.

"Even the Ways and Means Committee members," says one of them, "haven't the vaguest notion usually what the bill is about, let alone ordinary House members."

Legislators on the tax-writing committees are often under intense pressure to insert special provisions into a tax bill on the claim of inequity by some industry or individual, and they are often disposed, naturally enough, to be helpful. As a member of the Senate Finance Committee once said: "What's the good of being on this committee if you can't get through a little old amendment now and then?" But if the member is wise, he will first seek Stam's views.

Says a tax lawyer: "It is easy to pull a blooper, and the committee can then be made to look like an idiot. The fact that Stam can prevent that—and only Stam—gives him a tremendous hold over the committee."

This ability to steer the tax-writing committees away from folly and trouble has been especially important since the Ways and Means Committee in 1955 decided to allow each House member one technical amendment to be considered in committee and incorporated in the bill, providing it received the committee's unanimous approval.

Third, there is Stam's sixth sense for what will win the favor of the chairmen and ranking members of the tax-writing committees. From long association with them he can anticipate their attitudes toward Treasury proposals and their possible interest in a "relief" amendment pressed on behalf of a client by a tax attorney. As one lawyer said admiringly, Stam is not simply "cagey" in assessing the temper of important committee members, but he takes the initiative in calling "special interest" proposals to their attention and "in articulating their ideas and desires in technical terms."

To see how Stam exercises his knowledge and influence, it is necessary to trace briefly the course of a major tax bill.

The Constitution assigns to the House sole power to originate revenue bills. However, it is now established custom that legislative action on a major tax bill is set in train by the President's recommendations, either in the budget or in a special message. When the White House and Congress are controlled by the same party, the President and the Secretary of the Treasury will have conferred beforehand with the chairmen of the tax committees.

After receipt of the message, the House Ways and Means Committee chairman schedules public hearings. The Secretary of the Treasury—chief lobbyist for the administration—leads off, followed usually by the Director of the Budget and the chairman of the President's Council of Economic Advisers. Then comes a seemingly endless procession of witnesses—most of them attorneys—representing various sectors of industry and trade, labor, agriculture, consumer groups, individual companies, private (but usually large) taxpayers, and tax scholars. The witnesses may be there to support or oppose the President's main proposals—for example, dividend withholding or investment credit—or to plead for some "special provision," commonly known as a loophole, to redress what they believe to be some unfairness in the existing statute.

Even before the hearings start, Stam and his staff have swung into action, assembling data and analyzing the effects of the President's proposals. In this work, as Roy Blough writes in *The Federal Taxing Process*, "heavy reliance has come to be placed on the chief of staff, who determines the character and the viewpoint of the material presented by the joint committee staff."

As the hearings drone on and the testimony becomes repetitious and the witnesses less important, only the chairman and perhaps two or three other members are present. But Stam, or one of his principal aides, stays the course to answer questions when needed, but chiefly to get a sense of prevailing sentiment and hear arguments for special provisions that may be raised later in secret session.

In fact, all during this preliminary period, attorneys lay siege to committee members in behalf of clients. This is inevitable under a nonparliamentary system, since Congress is the mediator between the Executive and the demands of pressure groups. A tax attorney thus describes what happens:

"The congressman says to the lawyer, 'Go see Stam, and then let me get a report from Stam.' If Stam thinks there is no merit in the idea, the congressman will usually drop it. If Stam thinks there is merit, the congressman is likely to sponsor it."

Sometimes the procedure is reversed. "An attorney will call on Stam to tell him what he would like to do and see whether it is in the cards. Stam may say, 'Don't waste your time,' or 'You might be able to interest so-and-so in that.' If Stam himself is interested, he will explain the proposal to the congressman in friendly terms, without necessarily urging it, and so help put it across."

Open the records of public hearings at random, and it becomes apparent how much reliance the members place on Stam to supply both facts and guidance. The following two examples happen to be drawn from the 1951 Senate

Finance Committee hearings, but they could be duplicated from the House Ways and Means Committee hearings.

Here is John W. Hanes, president, Ecusta Paper Corporation, accompanied by Walter F. O'Connell, accountant, protesting "a very serious inequity" in the 1950 excess-profits tax law:

MR. O'CONNELL. The average earnings of the parent company are computed, and a credit is determined, and 12 per cent of any increase in inadmissible assets after the commencement of the excess-profits tax period is a reduction of the earnings credit as well as—

SENATOR TAFT. Is that so, Mr. Stam?

MR. STAM. Yes.

SENATOR TAFT. How does that work?

MR. STAM. You see, the parent is giving up something. . . . So that they have their capital reduced.

And here is Cyrus B. King, attorney, representing Wixson & Crowe Inc., of Redding, California, seeking relief:

MR. KING (concluding his argument). I have never felt that I have placed a matter before a tribunal from which I could expect better results than I do from you gentlemen. Thank you.

SENATOR TAFT. May I ask, Mr. Stam, has that question been up with your committee? Has it been up with your staff, Mr. Stam?

MR. STAM. We have discussed it with Mr. King, and we have the matter—

SENATOR TAFT. Do you see any particular reason why it should not be done? Is there any argument against it?

MR. STAM. I think it is a matter that we certainly should try to see if we cannot remedy without opening the door too wide in a lot of other cases. Of course, the whole problem where you have what we call a closed transaction is that where part of the assets go over and part are retained, you get into this question of a double credit; and that is, the old company continues to keep the credit and the new company gets the same credit, and we have tried to work out many of these tax-free exchange provisions under this particular section to keep the credit in the hands of just one taxpayer.

It is when the House Ways and Means Committee goes into executive session that the shirt-sleeve work begins. The members come down off their dais and sit around a U-shaped table, with the chairman in the center and the members of either party ranged to left and right in order of seniority. In the middle of the U, facing the chairman, sits Colin Stam. Attending are representatives of the Treasury, the Internal Revenue Service, the House Ways and Means staff, and the legislative counsel of the House who must do the drafting.

In effect, Stam is in charge of the proceedings. He is called upon to reply to the arguments of the Treasury representatives. He funnels material to the chairman. He feels his way, sensing out and proposing compromises. As one member describes the scene:

"Stam is usually called on for an opinion, and he is anything but shy or bashful. Since the House bill comes to the floor under a closed rule prohibiting all except committee amendments, all he has to have is influence over a majority of the committee."

As tentative policy decisions are reached, the staff of the legislative counsel begins the drafting, with attorneys

122 ★ Adventures in Public Service

from Stam's staff and the Treasury sitting in. Then comes the line-by-line vote in committee. Again Stam is on hand to supply last-minute advice.

Finally, Stam is responsible for the committee report on the bill. He himself usually prepares that part known as "the guff," which describes and justifies the bill in non-technical language, and estimates the impact on various taxpayer groups. The second part of the report containing a technical explanation of each section is left to the legislative counsel and the Treasury.

When the bill comes to the floor of the House, Stam sits beside the floor manager, usually the House Ways and Means chairman, so that he can be consulted when questions arise or if trouble develops. Under the closed rule, the bill rarely runs into difficulty.

Stam now puts on his Senate hat and accompanies the bill to the Finance Committee. The whole procedure is now repeated, with two important differences, both of which strengthen Stam's influence. First, the Senate Finance Committee is dealing with an actual draft of a bill and not a set of executive proposals. Most members want to alter the House draft in some way, and Stam is there to help them. Second, there is no limit to floor amendments, and therefore Stam is on almost constant call by the floor manager.

Finally the two versions of the bill go to a conference of selected members of the House and Senate committees. There Stam acts as explainer and catalyst.

"The problem of serving impartially the interests of both committees when they are on opposite sides of important issues," Dr. Blough writes, "has not been solved.

This fact has not prevented the Chief of Staff from exercising a profound influence over tax policy decisions."

Of all congressional staffs, with the possible exception of that of the Senate Committee on Foreign Relations, that of the Joint Committee on Internal Revenue Taxation has the most professional competence. This is Stam's creation. The members are not under civil service tenure, though they enjoy retirement benefits equivalent to those of the classified Civil Service. The committees have given Stam complete freedom to hire and fire and promote. He never inquires into the politics of a staff member before or after hiring.

In 1963 Stam had three assistants, seven attorneys, four accountants and statisticians, one economist, three consultants, and ten clerks. The attorneys are generally just out of law school and sign on for two years—Stam's minimum requirement—for the experience in tax legislation before joining a firm specializing in tax work. The other professional staff members usually remain for several years.

The late Senator Robert LaFollette, Jr., of Wisconsin was a member of the Finance Committee, and was so impressed with the Joint Committee staff that he drew upon it as a model for the staffing of standing committees when he and Senator (then Representative) Mike Monroney drew up their Congressional Reorganization Act in 1946.

Stam's relations with his staff are friendly but formal. He does not encourage familiarity. Men who have worked closely with him for twenty years still address him as "Mr. Stam." (A new member who once called him "Colin" was not rebuked but he was chilled.) Stam will put in an appearance briefly at an office party. But he does not entertain even his top assistants at his home, nor do they entertain him. His whole demeanor toward the staff is one of distant courtesy.

He is exacting without being tyrannical. He encourages senior staff people to assume responsibility and—up to a point—he accepts difference of opinion. There have been times when members have talked back to him without penalty because he valued their technical ability. He is a stickler for accuracy and takes no risks of error that he can forestall by personal attention. Thus he insists upon reading all letters before they are sent out and frequently challenges the drafter with, "I'd like to see the page and verse for that."

With some exceptions he has been tightfisted about salaries. He shares Senator Harry F. Byrd's sentiments on government spending and believes he should set an example in budget-peeling. He himself is paid $21,500 a year. No other congressional staff chief receives as much.

His colleagues respect his knowledge, his quick grasp of the most involved problems ("he is easy to brief," says one), his single-minded devotion to the job, his capacity for work, his loyalty to his principals, and his "total incorruptibility." Long before Senator Paul Douglas established the thirteen-pound ham as the outside limit of lagniappe that he could accept without fracturing his conscience or arousing suspicions of payola, Stam was returning—and directing his staff to return—Christmas booze. Years ago he was given an expensive brief case that he did not know how to return without seeming rude, because the donor had had his initials lettered in gold on it. He has never used the case, and to this day it lies slowly rotting in a corner of his office.

It must be recorded, however, that the respect in which he is held by his staff, and by many lawyers and legislators, is not tempered with affection. In part their reserve is a response to Stam's own lack of warmth. He seems neither to need nor want closer relationships than the efficient management of his office requires. Beyond his chilling aloofness, there is a quality of suspicion in Stam that inhibits friendships. He moves in a political atmosphere where clash of opinion is inevitable and where adjustment, compromise, and the dismissal of yesterday's differences are the pragmatic conditions of life. Yet Stam does not dismiss differences. He trains "an unforgiving eye" on proposals with which he disagrees, and tends to see a personal affront in views that clash with his own.

"In some ways," said one reporter who has watched him nurse old grievances for years, "he is a sad figure."

But against his behind-scenes harassments of officials and reporters who have incurred his displeasure must be set many unrecorded acts of kindness. Often he has come quietly to the rescue of a staff member who has been pinched for money in a personal or family crisis. For years he coddled along a staff assistant with a bad drinking problem, hoping that he would finally get him straightened around.

As he has grown older, Stam keeps more regular working hours. But in some big tax years, especially during World War II, he worked two and three nights a week, and every Sunday and holiday. This involved less sacrifice for him than for his staff. Tax law has been his life, and he has always been a bachelor.

He lives with two sisters—Miss Louise and Miss Susan —in a fairly large, colonial-style wooden house just across the District of Columbia line in Chevy Chase, Maryland. The rooms are filled with fine antique furniture. Stam reads history and historical biography, and he is an expert on the history of the Eastern Shore of Maryland where he was born. The Washington social round holds no attraction for him. In 1961 and 1962 he attended the annual dinner of the Saints and Sinners Club, at which a prominent official is made the "fall guy." He has occasionally shown up at a Christmas party of one of the prominent law firms, where he will take one or two sips of a drink and set it down.

He is also a nonsmoker, though he once chain-smoked for a good part of an afternoon. The occasion was a business visit to the State Department, during which a diplomat kept offering him a cigarette. Each time Stam took one and manfully smoked it. Later, when a colleague who had accompanied him asked why he had done this, Stam replied; "It was a matter of protocol."

Back in the Twenties Stam had a trim figure and played excellent tennis, standing fifth or sixth in the Capital's rankings. Now he is bald and bulky. At lunch he will adhere to a diet of cottage cheese and Jello, and then in the afternoon succumb to a compulsion for peanuts, candy bars, and Cokes.

One senator has likened Stam to "an unmade bed," and the stories on Capitol Hill of his absent-minded unkemptness are legendary. He once entered the House to see a member, and as he walked down the center aisle with his hat on, Speaker Sam Rayburn spied him and called out roughly that hats must be removed in the chamber. Stam, totally unaware that he was the offender, continued on his way, discussed his business, turned and walked up the aisle while "Mr. Sam," purple with anger, banged his gavel.

On another occasion Stam was expounding a difficult point of law before the House Ways and Means Committee. It was before the days of air conditioning, the day was warm, and members and staff had shed their coats. Not Mr. Stam. One of his aides noticed that—as so often happened—Stam's shirttail had worked its way out of his trousers and was hanging below his jacket. Quickly the aide went up to the table and whispered in Stam's ear. Without embarrassment or interruption of his discourse, Stam proceeded to tuck in not only his shirt but the whole rear of his jacket.

All might have been different if Stam had married. But as one congressman said, "He has never seemed to mind his single state. He has the same feeling toward the Internal Revenue Code that most men have toward their wives."

Ever since he became chief of staff in 1938, Stam has been a controversial figure in the profession. He has had his champions and still has them. But they have come mostly from the ranks of the law firms and the chairmen and ranking minority members of the tax committees whose names are a roster of fiscal conservatism—Senators Pat Harrison of Mississippi, Walter George of Georgia,

Eugene Millikin of Colorado, Harry Byrd of Virginia; and Representatives Robert (Muley) Doughton of North Carolina, Harold Knutson of Minnesota, Daniel Reed of New York, Noah Mason of Illinois.

The nonadmirers comprise a long list of past and present Treasury attorneys and economists who have gone into not-very-dubious battle against him ("If Stam is for something and the Treasury is against it, it usually gets in"), congressional liberals, tax professors, and financial reporters.

Almost without exception, his opponents pay ungrudging tribute to his abilities, his personal integrity, and his refusal to leave the public service for the fat consultant salaries of $50,000 and more a year he has been offered repeatedly. But all this weighs little with his detractors.

He has, they maintain, used his powers "negatively" to oppose Treasury proposals and has played a major part in defeating many of them. He leaves to the Treasury the task of speaking for tax equity and fairness. He is a man without a broad policy of taxation who yet makes policy. "If he has a 'philosophy of taxation,'" said one tax expert, "it is to serve the most powerful members of the committees." He knows little and cares less about the relation of taxes to economic and fiscal theory. He is generally unsympathetic to reform, uninterested in simplification, and prone to give the impression to influential law firms that they have a friend at court. These are the shortcomings that Stam's critics believe have marred his record as the principal advisor to the tax-writing committees.

Some exceptions need to be entered at this point. For example, in 1950 Stam supported acceleration of corpo-

rate tax payments although this was anathema to big business. And in the same year he got together with Treasury
on trimming the oil depletion allowance from 27½ to
15 per cent. (This idea was stillborn.) Again, he was for
payroll withholding in 1943—at that time a very controversial innovation. And he has taken a strong position
against allowing the "tax-exempts" to escape taxes on income from businesses they have purchased or received
from philanthropic donors. His argument is that tax exemption gives the owners an unfair advantage over competing firms that have to pay the regular corporate taxes.
(An example is Mueller's, the makers of macaroni and spa-
ghetti, all of whose stock was left to New York University.)

Stam's critics contend, however, that most of these exceptions hardly test the rule. For example, they note that
Senator George and Representative Doughton, then chairmen of the tax committees, also favored withholding. By
contrast, they recall that when Senator Harry Byrd in 1962
opposed withholding on dividends and interest, so did
Stam, though originally he had favored the Treasury proposal. Again they note that while Stam is all for closing the
loopholes enjoyed by the tax-exempts engaging in competitive business, he has been anything but zealous about a
whole range of notorious loopholes favoring business firms
and influential taxpayers.

Indeed, it is precisely here that his critics direct their
main charge: namely, that he has not only accommodated
himself to special-purpose legislation, and particularly
during Senator George's chairmanship, but has also at
times "created loopholes" that he has persuaded committee members to sponsor, knowing them to be predisposed

to the beneficiaries of such legislation, or sympathetic to its rationale.

In support of this argument, his critics like to cite the now-famous "Mayer amendment" of 1951.

Louis B. Mayer, who had been for twenty years vice-president in charge of film production for Metro-Goldwyn-Mayer, had had for twelve years a contract with his employer entitling him to 10 per cent of the net proceeds of every picture made by the studio between April 7, 1924, and five years after his retirement or until prior death.

On retirement in 1951, Mayer released his rights to the uncertain profits in return for a lump-sum payment of about $2,750,000. Under the normal 91 per cent top-bracket rate, comparatively little of this payment would have remained to Mayer after taxes. His problem was: How could this particular payment be made subject to the 25 per cent capital-gains tax? The Washington firm of Alvord and Alvord was engaged to try to find relief. Senators George and Taft proved to be sympathetic to Alvord's arguments, and the Finance Committee went along on a special provision duly drawn up by Stam's office to meet the exigencies and the particularities of the case, as follows:

> "Amounts received from the assignment or release by an employee, after more than twenty years' employment, of all his rights to receive, after termination of his employment and for a period of not less than 5 years (or for a period ending with his death), a percentage of future profits or receipts of his employer shall be considered an amount received from the sale or exchange of a capital

asset held for more than six months, if such rights were included in the terms of the employment of such employee for not less than twelve years, and if the total of the amounts received for such assignment or release are received in one taxable year and after termination of such employment."

Mr. Mayer saved an estimated $2 million.

In the 1954 code, the Mayer amendment was continued but its special intent was recognized by restricting its application to contracts entered into prior to that code.

It is the contention of Stam's critics that if he were "more concerned with the public interest," he would throw his weight *in camera* against weakening the tax fabric by such loopholes.

Before accepting such criticism, one needs to consider, in fairness, Stam's own conception of his role.

It is his view that he and his staff are there to serve the Joint Committee and not the Treasury, because the committee is the creation and instrument of Congress. More particularly, he believes it is his prime duty to serve the chairmen of the tax committees because they have risen to the chairmanship under the approved seniority rule. As one former official of the executive branch explains it:

"Stam is of that breed who says: 'My function is to bulwark the position of my principals.' He has two sets of principals who are frequently on opposite sides of the fence. He fortifies both. He will stand up and argue against the Treasury one way in the House and another way in the Senate. When a chairman wants support and another member wants information on the opposite side, he will provide the information, but not in public. He does not allow himself to be used to build a case against his principal."

This can be illustrated from the tax bill of 1962. Senator Byrd of Virginia opposed the investment credit as a "giveaway." So did Stam. (The investment credit provided that a firm could deduct from its tax payment 7 per cent of what it had spent during the year for new machinery and equipment.) Byrd was also against the Treasury's proposal for current payment of taxes on foreign-earned income instead of waiting for the repatriation of earnings. So was Stam. Although Stam initially favored dividend withholding, Senator Byrd preferred the device of "information returns" to be matched against actual returns. Stam also decided that withholding was too complicated and too great a burden on companies and banks.

Because he differed with the Administration, Senator Byrd turned over to the late Senator Robert Kerr the task of handling the hearings and managing the bill. Kerr knew Stam's views and did not want the Chief of Staff beside him on the floor. Nor did Stam want to be there. He deputized the staff economist, Larry Woodworth, to serve Kerr.

Stam has not regarded it as his function to try to mold congressional opinion in line with the Executive's views, or to try to impose on the committees any particular policy. Rather, he has seen his duty as accommodating and reflecting the views of the members who happened to be chairmen. Thus, said one lawyer, "if Walter Reuther took over the Ways and Means Committee, Stam would have no problem," adding that he might now have some problem because he has become more set in his ways.

Correspondingly, on the issue of special tax provisions, Stam believes it entirely proper to bring to the attention of committee members suggestions for relief in which they might be interested. In fact, in 1962 he had the staff prepare a pamphlet made up of such suggestions culled from the hearings.

If Stam is friendly to a firm like Alvord and Alvord and pays attention to what it pleads, this is not, a lawyer explains, because he is "playing footsie" with lobbyists, but because the firm often reflects positions akin to those of his chairmen. "Otherwise he would treat Alvord and Alvord as he does an attorney for the AFL-CIO." Another lawyer says: "Stam wasn't going to say the Mayer amendment was crazy if Taft or George was for it."

Stanley Surrey, one of the most eloquent opponents of special provisions (in fact, so forceful that the Senate Finance Committee gave him a very rough time at his confirmation hearings in 1961), has stated the Chief of Staff's position sympathetically, even though the love lost between the two men is negligible. Wrote Surrey in the *Harvard Law Review:*

"His role is a difficult and unenviable one. Many congressmen pass along to him the tax proposals that they are constantly receiving from their constituents. Undoubtedly, the chief of staff discreetly but effectively blocks many of these proposals from proceeding further. But he also, whatever his inclinations may be, cannot in his situation always say 'no.' Perhaps inevitably on the crucial issues his role tends to be that of the advocate of the congressman advancing a particular proposal on behalf of a special group. The special-interest groups cannot appear in the executive sessions of the committees, and the congressman sympathetic to their point of view is not technically equipped to present their case: he tends to look to the chief of staff to assume that task. Further, he looks to the chief of staff to formulate the technical compromises which will resolve the dispute between the special-interest group and the Treasury. The chief of staff must therefore work closely with the congressmen and be 'brilliantly sensitive to their views.' He must necessarily be able to gauge the degree of interest that a congressmen may have in a proposal and weigh that in the consideration of the guidance he will give. Because of these institutional pressures the chief of staff is very often the opponent of the Treasury Department before the tax committees."

Furthermore, among those high-minded men on Capitol Hill who have been most critical of Stam are some whose occasional lapses from grace hardly justify their retention of season tickets for seats of the scornful. Even sincere foes of special privilege have had a try at their own special-provision legislation.

Stam's influence reached its peak strength under Senator George and Representative Doughton in President Truman's last two years and during the writing of the 1954 code, which contained much new special-interest legislation. When the Democrats regained control of Congress in 1955, Jere Cooper, the new House Ways and Means chairman, did not make so much use of Stam and began building up a small professional staff for the Ways and Means Committee. In the Senate Finance Committee, however, which had almost no staff of its own, Stam's influence with first George and then Byrd was unimpaired. However, in the past two years, under the Kennedy administration, Senator Byrd's commanding position has been somewhat weakened—and Stam's power, too.

New problems require new approaches, and some committee members believe that Stam has become too inflexible, too unwilling to consider different viewpoints and too ready to arrogate to himself publicly a role in policy making that formerly he would have been content to exercise quietly.

For example, while some tax-writing committee members thought he was within bounds in compiling a pamphlet of proposed special provisions last year, they did object to his stating that these were staff "recommendations."

When Senator Douglas asked, with implied reproof: "Are you recommending these? What state do you represent?" Stam answered without batting an eye: "The United States."

A disinterested observer, with no emotional or intellectual involvement in tax legislation beyond surviving the April 15 deadline in a reasonably solvent condition, is baffled in trying to arrive at a fair assessment of Stam's influence over the years. And he will not get much help from the experts, for in this hypersensitive field all estimates of Stam seem polarized by the intensity of the emotions he has aroused.

On two things there is unanimous and unstinted praise. First, the codification of 1939 is a monumental piece of legal craftsmanship, for which he has deservedly won the gratitude of all who labor in this thistled field.

Second, Stam has done more than anyone to develop the committee staff system. This may well be his major and lasting contribution to government. But if this is to be his monument, it will, like the power he exerted, be anonymous.

Thomas B. Nolan

"I LOVE THY ROCKS AND RILLS"

GEORGE R. STEWART

THE TRUSTEES OF
PRINCETON UNIVERSITY

BY VIRTUE OF THE AUTHORITY VESTED IN THEM

UNDER A PROGRAM INITIATED BY JOHN D. ROCKEFELLER 3RD

TO STRENGTHEN THE CAREER

SERVICE IN THE FEDERAL GOVERNMENT

DO HEREBY GRANT A

ROCKEFELLER PUBLIC SERVICE AWARD

TO

THOMAS BRENNAN NOLAN

IN RECOGNITION OF DISTINGUISHED SERVICE

TO THE GOVERNMENT OF THE UNITED STATES

AND TO THE AMERICAN PEOPLE

Robert F. Goheen
PRESIDENT

Ronald B. Kipp
CLERK

DONE IN NASSAU HALL
PRINCETON, NEW JERSEY

THOMAS B. NOLAN

The relationship of a man and his institution—as of Thomas B. Nolan and the United States Geological Survey —is often complex. To examine it one must think almost in terms of ecology, of the interaction between an organism and its environment.

Emerson did not say the last word in his famous aphorism, "An institution is the lengthened shadow of one man." Critically considered, in fact, that saying is as inaccurate as it has been successful. The metaphor is distressing. Are we to consider that institutions project darkness, not light? Emerson, moreover, spoke with characteristic oversimplification.

If men create institutions, institutions also create men. Or, if they do not yet quite create them *ab ovo* (though that may be coming), they at least shape them to their final form.

Nolan did not create the Geological Survey. It had been functioning long before he was born. Still, he must be credited with some significant shaping of it, and because of him, its shadow (if we must use Emerson) will be the longer.

But the Survey has also to some extent created Nolan. Obviously, he was born without its help, and grew to manhood. Character and abilities being thus already formed, he would have been much the same man, and would probably have achieved an equally notable, although different, career in some other way if he had never joined the Survey. Still, the fact is, he joined it, and our present task here will be to examine something of what it has done for him and he for it.

The United States Geological Survey had its birth, after some peliminary travails, on March 3, 1879, when President Hayes signed the bill already passed by Congress. Although the Survey has the distinction of being our senior governmental scientific bureau, its foundation had a practical justification. In 1879 almost two fifths of our present area was still under territorial government, and therefore the direct responsibility of Congress. Even in many of the newly formed states, most of the land was federally owned. Moreover, many of these states were as scanty in finances as they were large in area, and no one could hope that they could get ahead rapidly with geological reconnaissances. Finally, much of this land had already produced gold and silver, and there was hope that it would produce, especially with scientific exploration, a much larger harvest of mineral wealth.

Under its first director (1879-81), the distinguished

Clarence King, and under its second director (1881-94), the even more distinguished John Wesley Powell, the Survey developed so rapidly and so successfully that we might think it destined to greatness from the beginning. Its first geologists, as we look back upon them now, seem almost like Homeric beings of larger stature than men. Such were G. K. Gilbert, I. C. Russell, S. F. Emmons, F. V. Hayden, Arnold Hague, and C. E. Dutton. That was the heroic age. Some of these men seem to have accomplished more singlehanded, traveling by pack train, than a modern team accomplishes with a helicopter and electronic instrumentation.

As it went along, the Survey had to create a policy for itself, and at the same time accept responsibilities for creating policy for the nation. Geology requires maps. There were no maps. Therefore the Survey had to make its own, and from this origin its topographical division has developed into a great map-making agency. On the other hand, when Congress became concerned with the arid regions and with the need of knowing what water was available, it passed this problem on to the Survey. And still a large proportion of the energies of the Survey is expended upon water resources.

An agency concerned with mapping the land was also in a good position to collect information upon what was growing on the land, even though trees and grass are not geological in the ordinary sense of the word. So Congress entrusted the Survey with this work, and only in 1905 was this responsibility moved to a new Bureau of Forestry.

Other offshoots from this "mother of bureaus" have been the Bureau of Reclamation (1907), the Bureau of

Mines (1910), the Federal Coal Commission (1922), and the Federal Power Commission (1930).

Obviously, all these achievements by the Survey have been accomplished by means of much brilliant thinking and even more hard work, and not without disappointments, heartaches, and some wrangling.

The fact remains that even on May 21, 1901, the Survey was already twenty-two years old, a well-founded and growing concern, proud of its record and of its established traditions. That particular day may be offered as an important date for the Survey—and also for Dr. and Mrs. Frank Wesley Nolan of Greenfield, Massachusetts. On this day a future director and a son to the Nolans was born. They named him Thomas Brennan.

He grew up in New Haven, Connecticut, and even in his school days was marked for leadership. To establish this fact, we may quote from a brief unidentified newspaper statement, presumably of the year 1918:

> Thomas B. Nolan of 59 Kimberley Avenue has been given the scholarship to the Sheffield Scientific School . . . .
> Thomas Nolan was considered the brightest man to be graduated, and aside from his studies was interested in athletics at the school. He played on the football team, was captain of the gun club and president of the School Circle, one of the honor societies of the school.

So our subject seems to be conforming to the great American stereotype "all-round" man. He so continued by going to Yale, which among all great American universities has traditionally attracted this type. From his boyhood, however, he had naturally felt the attraction of Yale.

Not only was it his home-town institution, but also his father had attended it.

In college he specialized in metallurgy, thus beginning a lifelong interest in metals. For experience, he spent one summer vacation at the copper mining camp in Kennecott, Alaska. In 1923, under the guidance of his professor, C. R. Longwell, he did some work on the geology of Nevada, thus initiating, when he was only twenty-two, his association with the region of the Great Basin. As an undergraduate he took up bridge playing as a relaxation, and he has been, ever since, an enthusiastic, devoted, and dangerous player. He ended his undergraduate career in 1921, receiving the degree of Ph.B.

He went on to graduate school in geology. Something of the Yale undergraduate lingered about him, and the denizens of the geological laboratories, in some surprise, watched him going off to football games in a coonskin coat. Still, neither the game nor the coat can have distracted him very much, for he advanced rapidly with his work. The northwestern portion of the Spring Mountains in southern Nevada attracted him for his doctoral dissertation. He completed his graduate work in three years, was granted the Ph.D., and in 1924 was ready to face the world.

He faced it first in California, that summer, as an assistant to his professor at Yale, Adolph Knopf. June 18, 1924, is thus to be marked as another important date in the history of the Survey, since on that day it acquired a new junior geologist, at $1,860 a year. Twelve days later, on July 1, this appointment was made more formal by Nolan's confirmation as a P-1, the beginning professional rank in the Civil Service ratings of that time. He was on the ladder, at the lowest rung. At that time the Survey had a permanent staff of only 900, and the annual appropriation was less than $2 million. Only four or five new geologists joined it in an average year.

So he began work with the Survey, and we are entitled to ask what appeal it made—and, in general, still makes—to a man looking forward to a career.

Like any young geologist with a Ph.D. in those days, and in these days, too, Nolan had come to a place where there was a three-way split in the road, and he must choose one. To be sure, the choice was not irrevocable, but it was nonetheless significant and important in a man's career.

First, there was the road leading to what may be loosely described as "commercial geology." This would mean, almost certainly, working for a big corporation. Most likely, such a career would be involved with the exploration for oil or for metal. The great advantage—or at least the possibility—would be financial. The salary would be good, and with success there would be almost no ceiling upon that salary, since an up-and-coming geologist might work into an executive position. Besides, there might be a chance to invest one's savings shrewdly on the ground floor. To hope for an eventual fortune was not unreasonable.

The disadvantages were many: No one could expect much freedom of action. A man did what the company needed done, and the end normally was profit, not pure science and the extension of human knowledge.

The second choice was university work. The advantages here were a maximum freedom of action and the opportunity to emphasize basic and theoretical research. A man must expect to put about half his time into teaching, and that could be rated an advantage or disadvantage, according to personal feeling. In university work, the salary would be comparatively small. Though there would be no actual prohibition of a man's making an investment as the result of his own specialized knowledge, most men expected to finish up with no more than what retirement pay the university might grant them.

Then, as a third choice, there was government work, particularly the Survey. Here salaries were somewhat comparable to those in universities, much lower than those in commercial work. There was a good deal of freedom of action and of opportunity for basic research—more than in commercial geology but less than in a university. There was actual legal restraint against making investments in any company dealing in mineral products. There was, however, no teaching load to be considered, and so the proportion of time that a man could spend upon research, even if he could not always choose what research he wished to do, was very high.

At any particular time the possibility of starting in any one of these three lines may be different. Sometimes, as in the Depression, a new geologist would be glad enough to get any kind of job, anywhere.

In Nolan's own case, an important factor was certainly the environment of the Yale Graduate School. Professor Knopf had served on the staff of the Survey since 1912; he always remained something of a Survey man at heart, and many of his Ph.D.'s went on to Washington. In fact, a stray Harvard man in the Survey about that time is said to have remarked: "All the big positions in Washington are held by Yale men, and the Harvard men are doing all the little jobs." (How things were to change at the national capital!)

In that summer of 1924 Knopf and Nolan ("a very good assistant," Knopf still recalls) worked south along the Mother Lode, through the old gold-mining towns of the forty-niners, from Plymouth to Mariposa. Conditions were primitive, by today's standards. By virtue of that summer, Nolan has a link with the giants of old time who might be said to have lived off the country. There were fairly good roads and fairly good automobiles in 1924, but the Survey had not supplied a car for this project. Knopf and Nolan had to make use of public transportation—when there was any. Sometimes they walked and sometimes they thumbed rides—though a working geologist at the end of the day is likely to be too dirty and too disreputable-looking for any motorist to pick up.

In summer the hills of the Mother Lode are crisp and golden with ripe grasses, and the New Englander looked upon them askance. When Knopf, a native Californian, went into ecstasy about a view, Nolan replied: "Yes, if it only were green!" (And this from a man who was later to become a dedicated Nevadan!)

Nolan thus began, as is to be expected, by serving as an assistant. A Survey man, however, scarcely thinks himself as even beginning to grow up until he has had his own project. Nolan's first opportunity came that fall, when he was sent out on a piece of work that he found far from congenial, since it did not call for a kind of geology in which he was particularly trained. He had to investigate the brines in the region of Great Salt Lake. Knopf counseled him that the best thing to do was to continue with the Survey, accepting this uncongenial work, doing it properly, and hoping for better things later.

The project turned out to be, as Nolan had feared, without much intellectual challenge. But every young man, at the opening of his career, is likely to be saddled with such routine assignments. The job, part of a broader investigation of the national resources of potash, was more physically than mentally demanding. The beginning geologist had to make many tedious hand-drillings into the hard-caked salt flats, to measure the thicknesses of the layers of salt and silt, and to obtain samples of brine for analysis.

The work was not without some hardship and even a touch of danger. In a small-tired and uncertain car of that era, Nolan had to drive about the treacherous desert, sometimes across sand, sometimes across the mushy surface of silt softened by infiltration of brine. At times a mine safety rail car, shunted onto a siding, served as a base of operation. When an emergency call took the car away, the young geologist was left homeless.

Still, Nolan did the work well, and the first entry in his bibliography reads (rather strangely, for an expert in metals) *Potash Brines Underlying Great Salt Lake Desert, Utah* (1927).

A better opportunity soon came, after an emergency had been created by the resignation of an older geologist. On July 12, 1925, when he was twenty-four, Nolan began work on the project that was to establish his reputation. He went to Gold Hill, a decadent mining district in Utah just southwest of the Great Salt Lake Desert, near the Nevada line. It was an area in which the New Englander would see few green hills, and a great many dust devils and mirages.

But the geology was both fascinating and complicated. Nolan, having already made a beginning with Knopf in California, here settled into a serious and long-continued (and apparently lifelong) study of metalliferous deposits.

At that time the Survey had a "big brother" system, by which each young man worked under an older one. Nolan was thus closely associated with H. G. Ferguson, who carefully and skillfully schooled him in geological techniques, and whose interest in the Great Basin reinforced Nolan's own rapidly growing fixation with that area.

This study of Gold Hill was no quick-come-quick-go enterprise. He worked there during three seasons, returning to Washington in the winters to do the paper work on this as well as on the Mother Lode and Great Salt Lake investigations. Although he published an abstract in 1928 and brief special articles in 1930 and 1931, Nolan continued to labor on the Gold Hill notes for several years. The task was too basic and important to be hurried. In the meantime he did other field work, and worked also at these notes. His name appeared as junior author to Knopf on *The Mother Lode System of California* (1929). Nolan's other half-dozen publications up to 1934 begin to indicate both his geological and his technical specialties. All of them deal with areas in Nevada and Utah, and nearly all are concerned with deposits of metallic ores.

Finally, in 1935, appeared the 200-page *Gold Hill Mining District, Utah*. Even today, according to what seems to be the general opinion of geologists, this work represents its author's greatest scientific contribution. Not only did it establish virtually all that anyone would wish to know about the district, but it also established a great deal in general about the geological processes by which mineral ores originate. It was thus not only of commercial importance but was, in addition, a significant contribution to pure science.

Nonscientists may be surprised that such outstanding work as this originated from a man only thirty-four years old at the date of publication. In general, however, experience is showing that the greatest scientific discoveries are made by those who are still comparatively young.

During these years Nolan had been going up the ladder —assistant geologist (1926); associate geologist (1929); geologist (1934). He had also become engaged to Maybelle Orleman, and on December 3, 1927, they were married.

Sometimes a learned social historian will consider, in a multivolume work, the influence of the wives of great men upon their careers—for good and for bad. In the case of Mrs. Thomas B. Nolan, a historian will have to concede, we may believe, the influence to have been good.

She is known as "Pete," not only to geologists of all specialties from pre-Cambrian to recent, but also to the world in general. She herself, in spite of the demands of marriage, managed to continue for many years her own brilliant scientific work in medical parasitology with the National Institutes of Health (United States Public Health Service). As a wife, she functions equally well in Washington and at the summer post in Eureka, Nevada, where she maintains an oasis for geologists almost perishing of thirst in the desert, and holds the home front while her husband is out peering down mine shafts, chipping the corners off rocks, or rescuing some young geologist marooned by a flash flood.

The Nolans' only child was born in 1937—also, a Tom. Like his father and his grandfather, he went to Yale. He has worked for the Newspaper Enterprise Association and as part-time editor of suburban newspapers near Washington, and seems to be destined for a career in journalism.

Any biographer attempting to get the "feel" of a man's life takes refuge in the orderliness of "periods." The period of Nolan's life that we have just been presenting begins with his coming to the Survey in 1924 and ends with the publication of the Gold Hill monograph in 1935. This is a period of straight-line development—the line, a sharply ascending curve. It seems simple enough in retrospect, though it probably did not seem simple to Nolan at the time. We have a young Ph.D., intelligent and creative, active and ambitious, managing in eleven years to establish himself professionally and to win a scientific reputation.

The next period, slightly shorter, comprises nine years, down through 1944. But this is a time of greater complication, less satisfactory for the biographer to present, and possibly less satisfying for the man himself to live.

There is nothing surprising in this. The decade itself, from the depths of the Depression almost to the end of World War II, was a disturbed one, and a great many men's careers were violently disturbed, or even ended. Moreover, at this time Nolan was reaching an age and rank that subjected him to time-consuming and sometimes frustrating responsibilities. No longer was he one of the junior staff, free to talk with his fellows about the obvious stupidities of the senior members who were running things. Now he is in process of becoming a senior member himself.

Yet he is not altogether in charge, either. Sometimes he must find himself in an embarrassing halfway position of a man whose opinion is asked and then perhaps ignored. Sometimes he must accept responsibility without having the power that should go with it. During these years he became known to his contemporaries and fellows as a man on whom they could count. He gave much and asked much. To younger professional colleagues for whose work he was responsible, he was a hard but friendly taskmaster.

He became known to members of the Survey generally as a man who could see where reforms were needed; as a crusader who could fight, with energy and courage, to accomplish what he thought to be needed; and as a good companion and brilliant cardplayer. Such a one could not remain the most placid of men. He was not beyond worrying, but usually he worked so many hours a day that there was little time left over for worry. Colleagues remember an occasional boiling-over, which they attributed to his Irish ancestry. (The present biographer, a descendant of Scots, does not see how, without race prejudice, he can be denied the same privilege, and hereby lays formal claim to it.)

Although Nolan had already established himself as a

great field geologist, the Survey came to make use, for executive ends, of his magnificent drive, his breadth of understanding, his endless capacity for detailed work, and his ability to handle people.

During much of this time he served as assistant to D. Foster Hewett, chief of the metals section, whose imagination previsioned the need of a vast strategic-minerals program, preparatory to what was to him the inevitable World War II. (Hewett became one of the Survey's grand old men, still actively at work in early 1963 at the age of eighty-two.)

Inevitably, as a direct result of planning for war requirements, scientific work paid the price. Although the counting of items is never conclusive, we may note that in Nolan's first period, ending in 1935, he published fourteen titles. In the second period, ending in 1944, he published only six.

The areas of concentration are the same—Nevada and Utah, and metalliferous deposits. More and more, though the bibliography before 1944 shows no evidence of it, he concentrated his field work upon the extensive and highly complicated mining region centering around Eureka, Nevada, where he began work in the early Thirties.

One contribution of this period is especially interesting as showing a new development in its author. This is *The Basin and Range Province in Utah, Nevada, and California* (1943). We can note in it the characteristic shift of the maturing scientist toward synthesis and the larger scope. The region here described extends over hundreds of thousands of square miles, and obviously could not possibly be studied in detail by one man, even if he did nothing else in his life. Nolan had made minute studies of several small areas of this region, and was more or less familiar with all of it. The monograph, however, is essentially a masterly review and appraisal of work already accomplished and available in the literature. It still remains, after twenty years, an invaluable work of reference.

During the wartime emergency with respect to strategic metals, Nolan was assigned tungsten as his special responsibility. Tungsten, so essential for the production of special steels, was in short domestic supply, and foreign production was largely in countries from which we could expect to be isolated in the event of war. The situation was so serious that to meet this and other demands for strategic metals Congress voted—for the first time in decades—significant increases of the Survey's budget.

In recruiting a group of brilliant young geologists to assist in the tungsten work, Nolan gave a fine display of his abilities at judging men. At the same time, in dealing with the War Production Board and other government agencies, he gained administrative experience and displayed himself efficient at such work. He emerged, no longer a "mere" scientist, but an executive who accomplished what he said he could accomplish, and got things done. Inevitably, it would seem—even, perhaps, against his own deeper desires—he was becoming known as an administrator.

As for tungsten itself, that metal had been mined at Gold Hill during World War I, and Nolan was therefore already familiar with the problems associated with its occurrence. As a result, he was rapidly able to become a leading authority on tungsten. Interestingly, not one of his published works deals chiefly with tungsten, and that word does not appear in any of the titles. We may assume that he wrote confidential reports, which may eventually become the basis for general works.

Three articles (1937 and 1938), all in collaboration with W. D. Johnston, Jr., show Nolan branching out into theory. Like architects, sculptors, oceanographers, and some other followers of the arts and sciences, geologists are "three-dimensional men." Printing, however, is two-dimensional. Thus the geologist always faces the problem of how to represent three dimensions when using only two, and the problem can probably never be solved to everyone's satisfaction. Nolan had been a pioneer (especially in *The Underground Geology of the Tonopah Mining District, Nevada,* 1935) in using block diagrams, and in these later reports, he and his collaborator were successful in combining plans and profiles to depict the underground rock structure as it would be revealed if segments of the earth's crust were removed and held up for inspection like separate pieces of pie or cake.

The final, and still continuing, period of Nolan's professional life began in 1944. Specifically, it was initiated, though without bad omen, on the shortest day or the year, December 21, when, on the recommendation of Director William E. Wrather, Secretary of the Interior Harold L. Ickes appointed Nolan to be Assistant Director of the Survey. He was then forty-three years old.

During his eleven years as assistant director, Nolan came to shoulder more and more of the general responsibilities. His final appointment as director, as with previous directors, followed a recommendation by a committee of the National Academy of Sciences, nomination by the President of the United States, and confirmation by the Senate. His shift to the directorship thus seems, in retrospect, to have been almost a preordained evolutionary step in his career, and was therefore accomplished with a minimum of shock, both to him and to his colleagues.

This latest and culminating promotion—and almost by definition the final one—occurred officially on January 27, 1956. It brought, incidentally, much satisfaction to a sometimes almost forgotten state. Senator George W. Malone of Nevada, in presenting the nomination to the Senate, commented upon his own pleasure in being able to introduce to his colleagues this distinguished government servant, who was also a citizen of Nevada.

In these higher positions, Nolan faced immediately one great problem. Previously he had remained a geologist in the broad but somewhat limited sense in which the term is used in the world generally. As assistant director and as director, however, he had to be equally concerned with all the activities of the Survey. Now he could no longer be absorbed merely with his own kind of geology and his own kind of geologist. Now he must also consider topographical mapping, water resources, and the classification of public lands. He could not play a favorite. He must listen to spokesmen for the four major fields of the Survey, study their projects, be responsible for the adjustment of rival claims in the light of practical possibility of appropriations by Congress, and finally, he must approve the budget. Necessarily, he became, in hours spent and in problems faced, less of a geologist and more of an executive. He became less involved with the men measuring strata or trying to determine the origin of pebbles, and came to have much more in common with the men who might be managing a corporation. He had, in short, suffered a common tragedy of success, as our civilization knows it.

This tragedy has, however, one mitigating factor. It often happens rather late in life, when the best creative ideas have already been reaped and when (in the case of a geologist, at least) the joints and the heart no longer feel the old pleasure in romping up and down Pliocene ridges.

But the whole problem is an important one in our civilization. It springs from a dilemma, and it is probably inescapable. To gain and hold the full respect of his colleagues, a man must be a professional leader, and this means that he must be outstanding in research. But to make such a man an executive means that he must give up, or nearly give up, his research. To this impasse the most painless solution occurs when a distinguished research man, nearing fifty, begins to recognize that new ideas come to him less often, and deliberately turns to executive work, realizing that he can still function in that field with the benefit of great accumulated knowledge and wisdom.

Nolan, at forty-three, was not one of these latter men; that is, he was not a man who was as yet slacking off in research, though he certainly was beginning to have the accumulated knowledge and wisdom. The problem of widening his interests to embrace all the fields of the Survey he met, apparently, with little difficulty. He was still young enough to make such a shift easily. Moreover, he soon seemed to impress his colleagues in the other branches with how much he knew about their fields and

how well he understood them. This breadth, in fact, remains one of his outstanding characteristics, to judge by
the comment that informed people make about him.

At the same time Nolan was still too young and much
too eager to renounce his scientific activities. Did he not
have a month's vacation every year? He began to turn this
into an extreme instance of the proverbial postman's holiday. Once the whistle blew for him in Washington, he and
Pete headed for Eureka.

There are few pairs of places in the United States that
offer greater contrast than do the national capital and the
old mining camp of Eureka, a few houses along U.S. 50,
in bleak and barren desert country, where nothing much
happens except when a tourist stops to buy gas.

The very change, doubtless, was part of the charm of it
for the Nolans. Soon they began to know the people and to
be themselves known. Eventually they established themselves as official residents of Nevada.

The life there fell into a pattern. Every year some young
geologist was assigned as Nolan's assistant. Daily the two
worked at the geology, either together (a safety factor
not to be neglected in that country) or each in a well-
defined area. In the evening they returned. The assistant
could then work on his notes or could go out, without loss
of face, on the unlikely chance that he might find some
amusement. But the Director faced a monumental pile of
mail and telegrams, which came to him even on vacation.
Almost normally, he worked late into the night, answering this correspondence by hand.

With a maximum of a month available yearly, the field
work went forward very slowly. Only in 1956 was Nolan

able to publish (in collaboration with C. W. Merriam and J. S. Williams) *The Stratographic Section in the Vicinity of Eureka, Nevada,* and not until 1962 the more definitive work *The Eureka Mining District, Nevada.*

Naturally, during this third period Nolan's published output fell off sharply. He did not publish at all between the years 1943 and 1950, in what should have been the rich harvesting time of his later forties. (Some of this gap may be attributed to wartime activities, but scarcely all of it.) During the nineteen years of his executive service, Nolan has actually been able to increase his bibliography by only twelve items. We must, of course, be amazed at how numerous they are, not at how few they are. Another significant fact must be noticed—only three can be called strictly scientific. The others, though making use of his broad professional attainments, are general, sometimes even approaching the popular. What has happened is clear enough, and it is common enough. It is part of our way of life, and no individuals can well go against its current. By and large, it is probably good, but it also involves various dangers.

Necessarily, a chief executive becomes involved with policy and policy making. Soon he finds that he must develop a long-range policy, and that to do so he must become something more than a scientist. He must develop a social point of view as well as some feeling for "good" and "bad"—words not commonly considered to be scientific.

Moreover, pressures in the same direction come from the outside. The chief executive is no longer to be considered a quietly retired scientist: he is a public figure. He receives invitations to speak from various organizations, and some of these he must accept. To unspecialized audiences, he must present the broader aspects of his topic. Even when fighting before a committee for his appropriation, the chief executive must emphasize the more humanistic aspects of his program. Perhaps, if we may so venture to put it, he must once again become something of the all-round boy of high school and the undergraduate in the coonskin coat in order to make contact with the unspecialized, nonscientific world. Even more, he must sometimes be the cardplayer.

Up to 1950, all of Nolan's publications are classifiable as scientific papers, usually of a highly specialized character. *The Search for New Mining Districts* (1950) is perhaps the first indication of something new. It is more definite in *The Outlook for the Future—Non-renewable Resources* (1955). Here we have even that generally nonscientific word "future."

In developing what we may call a social philosophy, Nolan has displayed an interesting outburst of optimism, which some have attributed to his Irish ancestry. He started, naturally, with his own specialties: ore deposits. His long-continued studies indicated to him that the amounts of metal still available are vastly greater than had once been supposed, and are, indeed, vastly greater than anything that has hitherto been exploited. Holding such belief, he could naturally develop an optimism with respect to the future of the human race, at least as far as his own special field might be concerned.

His point of view is perhaps most vividly expressed in *Use and Renewal of Natural Resources* (1958). In it he considers, half a century later, the conference on conservation called by President Theodore Roosevelt in 1908. That conference was a gloomy one in its predictions of coming scarcity and even depletion of mineral resources. Nolan points out that these prophecies were wrong. He then (blithely undeterred by the sad fate of the previous prophets) proceeds to prophesy on his own part that things in our future are going to be a great deal better.

Well, so may it be! The present biographer, however, perhaps because of his Scottish ancestry, feels himself bristling a little. Nolan, he thinks, has not given enough consideration to the situation outside the United States, where many countries are already in dire need of mineral resources. Moreover, the problem of population increase has been mentioned only to be lightly passed over.

The reader may not think the present biographer's opinions are of any importance in this matter. Yet perhaps they are. The writer here represents the layman. When a great scientist moves into general fields, he partially lays aside the armor of his specialty and becomes vulnerable to the judgments of those who are not specialists, or who may be specialists in other fields. It is a hazard that is to be manfully assumed when anyone moves along the road of scientist–executive–public figure.

Let all that pass. Certainly the chief problems of the Director have remained scientific and technical. Geology, like almost everything else, has been caught up in the atomic age and the space age. For some years the geological aspects of the search for uranium absorbed a large part of the activities of the Survey. The Survey has also moved out into fields that would leave King and Powell, its founding fathers, breathless. The study of the geology of the ocean bottom is now a flourishing project. So is the study of the geology of the surface of the moon. There is even a new conception of astrogeology. An interest in underground explosions has given a new stimulus to the old subject of seismology.

While these problems originate almost anywhere in governmental circles, they become particular problems of the Director himself. He must give the final yes or no, and thus must have some fundamental knowledge upon which to base his decisions. The directorship has not been, during Nolan's incumbency, a position in which any man could settle back comfortably into the well-earned rest of long service and approaching retirement.

There is, I think, no fourth professional period in view in Nolan's life as yet. But perhaps we should note a slight change in the last few years, as Nolan has gradually entered what we may call the period of awards and honors.

As a quite young man, in 1933, he received the Spendiaroff Award from the XVI International Geological Congress. As the years have passed, the honors have come more thickly—election to the National Academy of Sciences, the American Philosophical Society, and the American Academy of Arts and Sciences; and to the presidency of the Society of Economic Geologists and the Geological Society of America. In 1954, for his work upon tungsten, he received the K. C. Li Medal ($1,000), conferred by Columbia University. In 1961 he received the Rockefeller Public Service Award. On June 27, 1962, he went to Scotland for the granting of the degree Doctor of Laws, *honoris causa,* by the University of St. Andrews.

Undoubtedly there will be other awards. The story cannot yet be brought to a close. There will be further years, we trust, in the active directorship, and then a longer period during which, no longer active, he will still remain to be consulted as the elder statesman. There may well be a decade or two of summers, still, at Eureka. . . .

We must, however, take leave of our subject, in turning for a moment to that idea with which we began: that relationship between a man and an institution.

The Survey was twenty-two years old when Thomas Nolan was born. It was forty-five years old in 1924, when he joined it as junior geologist. It was seventy-seven years old in 1956, when Nolan, himself aged fifty-five, became its director. We have viewed his career with the Survey, breaking it down into three periods.

The Survey has given Nolan his opportunity for a career. He has been "a Survey man" par excellence. His career illustrates the possibility offered in government service for the outstanding man of science, especially if he also possesses executive abilities.

On the other hand, Nolan has contributed to the Survey. His scientific triumphs and honors have reflected light upon it. During his years of service the Survey has grown greatly in size and, even more strikingly, in complexity. The 900-man agency of Nolan's youth has expanded until, by 1962, it had 7,400 permanent employees. Of this army of workers, 1,150 were geologists, 310 were chemists or physicists, and 1,120 were topographic or hydraulic engineers. The Survey was spending $50 million a year from its direct appropriations plus $15 million transferred to it from elsewhere in the government. Especially during the recent years of Nolan's directorship, its growth has reflected the demands made upon it by other government agencies, notably by those concerned with nuclear science and outer space.

The Director has met these challenges and has grown along with his institution. He has continued to show outstanding ability at the task of understanding and appreciating the ever-increasing and ever more complex fields of endeavor that must be unified. But he has never relaxed his demands for individual excellence.

At sixty-two, Tom Nolan remains a vigorous personality, both physically and mentally. A tailor might sum him up as "size forty-two, stocky." A portrait painter would note his pink skin, bushy gray eyebrows, thick-lensed glasses, and full head of gray hair. He is quiet in speech and manner, with a twinkle in his eyes. He is a good listener, becoming impatient only, as a friend has remarked, "in the presence of illogical, or incorrect, or improper, or ill-mannered speech." In general, his reticence has become proverbial around the Survey.

People remark about him an intensity of manner that never leaves him, even when he is in his happiest mood at a gathering of family or intimate friends.

Friends he never gives up or lays aside. His attitude toward his hats is the same: he never gives up or lays aside an old one—much to his wife's distress at times.

Both physically and morally he is a man of courage. When his plane made a forced landing because of engine fire, he assisted the other passengers to escape, and then slid down a rope to the ground. He thereupon took the next plane. Similarly, when dealing with Congress, the Bureau of the Budget, or the Department of the Interior, he has stuck to his convictions in the face of strong opposition. He has also stanchly defended subordinates who have come under fire.

Hobbies of his earlier days still remain with him— bridge playing, stamp collecting, and bird watching. To the last he is particularly devoted, and may be declared an expert.

First and last, however, we can think of him as "a Survey man." Though John Wesley Powell still remains the archetypal shadow-throwing original, those in a position to warrant their having an opinion are already beginning to say that Nolan has to be ranked second only to Powell.

Perhaps, in the long run, his greatest contribution to the Survey will prove to have been his persistence in demanding professional standards. In words taken from the citation for his degree at St. Andrews: ". . . he has always demanded and consistently maintained [in the Survey] qualities of excellence which have come to be taken for granted by those who rely on its work."

Robert H. Felix

OUT OF THE SNAKE PIT

HERBERT C. YAHRAES, JR.

THE TRUSTEES OF
PRINCETON UNIVERSITY

BY VIRTUE OF THE AUTHORITY VESTED IN THEM

UNDER A PROGRAM INITIATED BY JOHN D. ROCKEFELLER 3RD

TO STRENGTHEN THE CAREER

SERVICE IN THE FEDERAL GOVERNMENT

DO HEREBY GRANT A

ROCKEFELLER PUBLIC SERVICE AWARD

TO

ROBERT HANNA FELIX

IN RECOGNITION OF DISTINGUISHED SERVICE

TO THE GOVERNMENT OF THE UNITED STATES

AND TO THE AMERICAN PEOPLE

PRESIDENT

CLERK

DONE IN NASSAU HALL
PRINCETON, NEW JERSEY

ROBERT H. FELIX

As the sun dropped below the wheatlands the Model T jounced to a stop and a man carrying a black bag stepped down and hurried into the farmhouse. A youngster of perhaps seven or eight followed. Later they came out and walked hand in hand around the yard.

"Son," the man said, "this lady is going to die."

"Can't you do something about it?" the boy asked.

The man explained why he could not: a Fallopian tube had ruptured even before he had been called, the lady now was in deep shock, it was too late to operate.

"I want you to think about this," he said. "Think about her husband and her two little children. Think what it means for this lady to leave them. And think about her, lying in there, a living person, conscious, but tomorrow . . ."

Put to bed on a downstairs sofa, the boy was awakened

in the night by the sound of crying. "We can leave now," his father told him.

"Don't they need us any more?"

"No, son. The neighbors will be in."

They drove home through the blackness.

"I want you to think about this." The man who often voiced this request as he traveled from patient to patient in Osborne County, Kansas, during the 1910's with his first-born child was the remarkable T. Ovid Felix. He had started his career as a Congregational minister, gone back to school and majored in history, earned a Ph.D. at Heidelberg, become a teacher, and finally, having fallen in love with a doctor's daughter whom he could not hope to support on a teacher's salary, had gone through medical college and become an M.D.

The boy who was solemnly urged to think about something—a death that came too early, the sounds heard through a stethoscope, the breath odor characteristic of a certain disease—was known throughout most of Osborne County as Little Doc. People took it for granted that he, too, would become a physician. He almost strayed into journalism, but in the end became an illustrious member of one of the least understood but most important branches of medicine.

An associate recently referred to Robert H. Felix as "Mr. Psychiatry." If this name fits a psychiatrist who can practice his profession only at odd hours, it is appropriately applied to the Little Doc who grew up to be the powerful head of the powerful National Institute of Mental Health.

If you know that at one critical point he was bent on

specializing in obstetrics, it may seem odd that he should be where he is. But there were strong factors impelling him both toward success and into psychiatry. A decision to enter the Commissioned Corps of the United States Public Health Service placed him on an escalator that can take one to high places if, in addition to staying power, one has brains and a knack for running things. The decision carried Felix to the equivalent of a rear admiral in the Navy or of a major general in the Army and has given him, since 1944, principal responsibility for the vastly expanding federal program for mental health. No one wields more influence than Felix on what is being done to combat mental illness.

The National Institute of Mental Health (or NIMH), over which he presides, is one of nine National Institutes of Health that make up the research bureau of the United States Public Health Service. The Public Health Service, in turn, is the largest of the five constituent agencies of the Department of Health, Education and Welfare. During the Felix era, the federal government's mental health budget multiplied a hundred times, from less than $2 million to $190 million for the fiscal year 1964 (compared with $145 million for the National Cancer Institute and $134 million for the National Heart Institute). The house that Felix built had become so large that moves were begun to detach it from the other eight institutes and make it a separate bureau, thus giving it still more influence and prestige.

In 1963 President Kennedy sent a message to Congress calling for a revolutionary new approach to the treatment of the mentally ill. Mental retardation and mental illness, the President told Congress, "occur more frequently, affect more people, require more prolonged treatment, cause more suffering by the families of the afflicted, waste more of our human resources, and constitute more financial drain upon both the public treasury and the personal finances of the individual families than any other single condition." The President's message noted that the nation's 279 state mental hospitals were currently sheltering more than 500,000 patients. In most of these hospitals, fewer than half the patients were receiving active treatment. Locked wards were the rule rather than the exception. Three fourths of the state mental hospitals had been opened before World War I. Nearly a fifth of them constituted fire and health hazards. As one of the major remedies for such conditions, the President recommended the creation of community health centers, with federal help, so that mental illness could be treated and prevented as other kinds of illness are treated and prevented—right in the community where it occurs.

President Kennedy justified the new mental health program by asserting that within a decade or two it would reduce the number of mental patients under custodial care by at least 50 per cent. Dr. Felix had gone further. "If communities assume the role that they and only they can play in building strong mental health programs," he said in 1962, "mental hospitals as we know them today will have ceased to exist within twenty-five years."

Felix has been driving toward comprehensive community mental health centers for many years. These centers, as the President's program provided, might be newly set up, or created by expanding existing mental health clinics, general hospitals, or mental hospitals. They might be sponsored by local governments, by state governments, or by voluntary, nonprofit organizations. The federal government would help to finance the planning of centers and, when the plans were approved, would contribute from 45 to 75 per cent of the construction costs. During the first few years of the program, the government would also help to meet the costs of staffing the centers.

What would be the advantages of such centers over the old hospital system? Dr. Felix explained that ". . . located in the patient's own environment and community, the center would make possible a better understanding of his needs, a more cordial atmosphere for his recovery, and a continuum of treatment. As his needs change, the patient would move without delay or difficulty to different services —from diagnosis to cure to rehabilitation—without need to transfer to different institutions located in different communities."

The centers would be accessible to everybody. An emotionally upset or mentally ill person could walk into a center by himself. Or he might be referred by his physician. Studies by Dr. Felix's Institute have shown that a large proportion of persons needing help can be successfully treated on an outpatient basis—while living at home. But if a patient needed hospital care, whether in the daytime or at night or around the clock, the center would take care of him. It would also arrange foster-home care; it would provide rehabilitation; it would offer consultant services to schools, courts, and welfare agencies, both public and private. It would be equipped to deal with a variety of problems: neurosis, psychosis, alcoholism, drug addiction, and mental retardation. And in many cases, the center could offer help so promptly that the patient would not need to be hospitalized. The aim, in short, would be to treat a person quickly and get him back to duty.

Under the new program, said Felix, ". . . we can return the mentally ill to the community. We can retain them in our communities. We can restore all but a small proportion of them to a socially productive life." He cited many examples, including that of a hospital in Massachusetts that successfully treated in the community one half of the mental patients for whom admittance had been sought.

A revolution in the treatment and prevention of mental illness, far from just beginning, however, has been long under way. A good starting date is 1946, when Congress passed the Mental Health Act, authorizing the Public Health Service to subsidize training in the mental health field, to increase the support of mental health efforts in the states, and to undertake and support research looking toward the causes and cures of mental illness. Felix, then forty-two and new head of the Public Health Service's Mental Hygiene Division, predecessor of the Institute, had had an important hand in shaping the legislation; many of his hopes for the country's welfare, and a few for his own career, were tied up in it. But the day after the President signed the act, Congress went home without voting an appropriation so that something could be done about it.

"You'll never get the money you need," some of Felix's colleagues warned, "unless somebody discovers a germ that causes schizophrenia."

Felix shrugged off the pessimists, and, hat in hand, visited a string of foundations until he found one that would give him $15,000 so that the National Mental Health Advisory Committee authorized by the act—and appointed by Surgeon General Thomas Parran, one of the great names in public health history—could convene and chart a program.

In those days, people by and large distrusted psychiatry and tended to poke fun at its practitioners, of whom there were distressingly few—as, indeed, there were of all types of workers in mental health. The accepted way of handling an emotionally ill person was to get him into a state hospital, generally far from home and friends, where, unless he recovered fairly soon, he might be moved into the back wards where recovery was almost impossible. Twenty-three states had not a single mental health clinic; the country as a whole had fewer than 500, clustered in the largest cities. Research was fairly meager.

By contrast, in 1963 every state had mental health clinics, and the nationwide total had more than tripled. The number of people with recognized graduate training in the principal mental health professions—psychiatry, clinical psychology, psychiatric nursing, and psychiatric social work—had grown from 12,000 in 1950 to more than 30,000. A large number of scientists, almost certainly running into the thousands, had been attracted to research in the field of mental illness. There were 132,000 fewer people in the state mental hospitals than there would have been had the number of patients continued to grow as in the years before 1956. During 1962, some 665,000 psychotic individuals were treated in mental health clinics;

more than 200,000 psychiatric patients were treated in general hospitals—and discharged as cured.

The advances, though certainly not attributable to NIMH alone, would have been considerably smaller had it not been for the money directed by the Institute into training and research programs, into state and community hospital and clinic projects, into medical colleges for the improvement of their psychiatric departments, and into a variety of grant and fellowship programs to train more people both for service and for research.

In 1963 Senator Lister Hill asked Felix to "give us the doxology" at the close of three days of hearings on bills to promote community mental health centers and to combat mental retardation. When Felix had finished, the learned Senator, Chairman of the Senate Committee on Labor and Public Welfare, quoted Emerson's familiar words: "An institution is but the length and shadow of an individual," and went on to say: "Here is the head of the National Institute of Mental Health, and what you have just commented on shows this wonderful leadership there."

"Sir," replied Felix in all humbleness but with customary facility, "shadows are cast by light, and were it not for the glowing light that comes from this house and the House of Representatives, I would have no shadow at all."

The truth was in both the Senator and the psychiatrist.

Robert Hanna Felix—the first two names honor an ancestor who fought in the Revolution—is a broad-shouldered, square-faced man of medium height but impressive appearance. Because there is generally a gleam in his brown eyes and about him a vibrant eagerness like that of a schoolboy late on a spring afternoon, people are inclined to doubt that he really does date back to 1904.

Some of his friends know him as "the Kansas windstorm," and his wife once confided that Bob had made no great impression the night they met when she was a nurse and he a resident in psychiatry—because, she had thought, he talked too much. But Felix's talk is generally both purposeful and effective; it charms congressmen, soothes committees, placates those whose requests he must turn down, enlightens dozens of audiences across the country, and has made his Sunday morning discussion group at St. John's Episcopal Church, Norwood Parish, Chevy Chase, Maryland, by far that church's largest.

Dr. Lawrence Kolb, who recommended that Felix succeed him as chief of the Division of Mental Hygiene, testifies that he was impressed by Felix from the start because the young doctor not only had a fine knowledge of psychiatry but also could impart it.

After Felix had graduated from the high school of Downs, Kansas, a railroad division point of perhaps 1,800 people in the north central part of the state, he matriculated at the University of Missouri, intending to study journalism. A deep interest in medicine had been instilled in him both by nature and nurture—the family had half a dozen doctors in addition to his father—but his mother had always wanted him to be, if not a clergyman, a journalist. Besides, his father had talked to Bobby not only of medicine but also of history, botany, ecology, and etymology. In addition, the boy had won several essay-writing contests, one of them a statewide affair asking entrants "to paint a picture in words so clearly that readers will see it"; his subject had been a Kansas sunset.

"There have been two great passions in my life," Felix has said, "—people and words. I have always liked to write, and I like to talk to people."

Instead of going to Missouri after high school, Felix contracted typhoid fever and nearly died. When he was on his feet again, he got a job in a grocery store and looked dreamfully to Christmas, when his girl would be home from Kansas State. But when Christmas arrived, the young lady was clearly not as warm as she should have been, and Bobby's kiss landed behind her ear.

"I have been away to college," she explained, "and I have seen polish. The rough corners have been knocked off me. I don't want to see you any more: it's no fun."

Looking back recently, Felix said he could not blame her. Though he had been president of his class during both its junior and senior years, and a good runner, he had always been small and unable to outfight people physically or get anywhere in football. At the time, he was crushed. "I decided that, by God, I was going to live to see the day when that girl would write and tell me she was proud to have known me."

The letter came in 1961, shortly after the Downs, Kansas, *News and Times* reported that a local boy who had risen to be Director of the National Institute of Mental Health had now won the Rockefeller Public Service Award. The woman wrote that she would always remember with pride that she had been Bob's girl in high school.

Felix entered the University of Colorado in 1922, having given up Missouri because his classmates from home would have been a year ahead. At the end of the first term, the dean called him in and pointed out that while he was doing excellently in chemistry and mathematics, he was almost flunking English, a subject Bob knew so well that he had rarely bothered to look at the textbook. Switch to zoology, the dean advised, and make up English in the summer. Bob assented, thereby depriving journalism—in view of Felix's energy, interest in people, and gift of gab —of a likely successor to one of his mother's heroes, Richard Harding Davis. For the zoology course was taught by a great geneticist, the lanky, bearded Dru Allison Cockerell, and Felix, fascinated, drew an A-plus. The next year he decided to major in biology and become a teacher; then he announced his intention of going to the university's college of medicine in Denver.

At medical school he soon ran into money trouble. He needed a microscope and secured it, easily enough, by selling the $100 trumpet he had earned during high school days so he could play in the orchestra. But he also needed a steady job. When the dean heard of the predicament, he asked Felix if he required much sleep.

"Not much, sir," Felix replied, "but I do need about four hours," whereupon he was named night driver of the university hospital ambulance. His hours were from seven to seven, and classes began at eight, but he could sleep between calls and had every other week end off. His pay was room, board, and laundry, and the room, wonderfully, was in the interns' quarters.

As a medical student and as an intern, Felix found with

some distress that he was taking a personal interest in every patient. "I would advise every young student in medicine," he said recently, "to remember that to die with every patient, or to suffer with every patient—you can't do it, you just can't do your best this way. Nonetheless, I found I could not get over wondering about these people —what they were being treated for, how they lived at home. That man who came into the hospital to get ready for an operation: last night his family had a meal together —sort of held each other's hands and hoped they would be together this time next year—maybe said a prayer.

"It seemed to me as I went along," he continued, "that the really happy profession was obstetrics. You'd go into the room as the mother was getting ready to leave and you'd say, 'Well, I'll see you this time next year.' And she would say, 'Oh, no, no, you won't—I've had enough.' And you'd laugh and say, 'What are you going to do—get a divorce?' or some other crack. And she'd come back in a few months and say, 'I wanted to show you the baby you delivered,' and then in a year or so she'd come back again and—. Well, this was a happy specialty.

"But as time went along, I found that even in obstetrics every now and then something dark appeared. In some of these cases—I had three of them within a couple of months—the mother developed what we called a post-partum psychosis. Within a few days of the birth, she'd be completely psychotic, and I couldn't understand it. My professor who had taught me in psychiatry—Dr. Frank Ebaugh—would come over and talk to her and then tell me things about my patient I didn't know. I was completely provoked. One day, as part of our training in medical school, we went for a visit to the state hospital—the old kind of state hospital that they had in the 1920's. There were long galleries, and patients would sit there in their rocking chairs—sit and pick their fingers, pick their noses, wet themselves. It was a kind of grim thing. It smelled, yes it did.

"As we left that day," Felix continued, "a number of my classmates said: 'Well, that's one thing I know damned well I don't have to worry about—being a psychiatrist.' My own reaction was different, thanks to something or other in my background. I kept thinking: If this is illness, and illness it is, there is a cause; and if there is a cause, there is a way of interposing measures either to prevent or restore. I still wanted to be an obstetrician, but I didn't have that general feeling against being a psychiatrist."

The doctor was sitting in his office overlooking the NIH campus as he recalled those early days. Suddenly he jumped from 1931 to 1963. "I still have to go to state hospitals—every few weeks or months," he said. "Many of them are much different now; maybe I had a little hand in it—I hope. But a lot of them are much as they used to be. Recently I walked into a hospital not too far from here and I smelled that smell. It stuck in my throat. I've been in psychiatry over thirty years, but I cannot experience these things and eat a good meal. You see a person with those vacant eyes and bizarre behavior and you wonder about that day long ago when some mother had that little red infant put in her arms. She would look at him with love and pride and wonder whether he was going to be a president, a senator, a scholar, or what. And here he is to-day—a vegetable. It just shouldn't be."

Owing partly to his compassionate nature and partly to the disturbing evidence that physicians trained in psychiatry could open some doors that others could not, young Dr. Bob turned down a residency that would have led to specialization in obstetrics, and accepted instead a Commonwealth Fund fellowship in psychiatry. He chose to take his three-year residency at the Colorado Psychopathic Hospital, the director of which was the same Dr. Ebaugh who had taught him psychiatry in medical school.

Felix says that his life has been shaped most strongly by his father and three other men—Ebaugh, Kolb, and the late Alan Gregg of the Rockefeller Foundation, who, as an old hand at distributing millions for medical research, impressed on the new hand the need for complete scientific freedom and passed along certain other valuable ideas on how to give away money. Of these three men, the one with the most influence appears to have been Ebaugh, who fervently believed that mental health was a community affair. He operated a psychiatric outpatient clinic at the hospital, which was unusual enough in those days, and also a network of traveling clinics covering the state. The residents in psychiatry—that is, doctors in training to become psychiatrists—would visit their assigned clinics several times a month, see patients from the area round about, and consult with the local doctors. Ebaugh had also introduced refresher courses in psychiatry for general practitioners, an idea now heavily backed throughout the nation by Ebaugh's student.

Dr. Ebaugh has recalled that Felix "would ask me the cause of schizophrenia [to the finding of which Felix's Institute allots millions of dollars a year] and push me regarding definitions of everything." Like himself, said the professor, Felix was "a classical hypomanic," a person with a drive lower than that associated with mania but considerably higher than average.

One evening in the fall of 1932 during his Colorado hospital residency, Felix was dancing with the slim and dazzling brunette who wore his ring—Peg Wagner—when she gave a little cough and noticed on her handkerchief a fleck of blood. "In Colorado, where tuberculosis was almost a commodity," Felix relates, referring to the fact that people flocked to that state to be cured, "I was scared to death." As it turned out, rightly so.

When he went to see her in the hospital the next day, she pulled off the ring and handed it to him. "You can't marry me now," she said. "I'd be a drag on you."

"You want to make me mad?" Bob asked. "Suppose this had happened six months after the wedding: I'd have been stuck with you, wouldn't I? You would have said to yourself that he's making the best of a bad bargain, and you would always have wondered what I would have done if we'd known about it earlier. So maybe kind Providence has done something for us. I don't have to marry you now: you've handed me back my ring. Now I'm telling you to put that ring back on, and don't ever try a thing like this again."

Characteristically, Bob insisted that they be married on the very date planned, June 18, no matter what. After the ceremony, held appropriately at Loveland, Colorado, in her sister's home, they ran out to the car, ducking handfuls of rice, and drove slowly around two blocks. Then they returned and the bride, exhausted, went to bed.

Two months later Felix finished his residency, accepted a commission as assistant surgeon in the Public Health Service—a strictly temporary means of earning his livelihood, he thought—and was assigned to Springfield, Missouri, where Dr. Kolb had just opened the Medical Center for Federal Prisoners. Peg was well enough to join him the following spring.

After eleven years of college, medical school, and postgraduate training, Bob now ranked with a lieutenant j.g. in the Navy, wore a similar uniform, and drew $262.66 a month. The Depression was at its depth, and he thought he had been handed a pretty good deal.

As a psychiatrist to convicts, Felix found himself puzzled by two questions. First, how much should you do for a man who is serving life, or double life, and who develops a psychosis and thinks God comes to see him every day, and this makes him deliriously happy? Second, just what was it that had made these prisoners, particularly the young ones, sin against society?

He did not succeed in answering either question to his own satisfaction, but the second strengthened an interest in sociology, which became manifested in NIMH's broad support of sociological research, including investigations into why boys go wrong and what makes successful adolescents successful.

After two years as practicing psychiatrist, Felix was promoted to be clinical director of the hospital and has never since been able to get away long from administration. Dr. Kolb, who had been moved from Springfield to open another new hospital—at Lexington, Kentucky, for persons addicted to narcotics—called him there in 1936.

Felix moved right up, from staff psychiatrist to chief psychiatrist to clinical director to executive officer. Better than these advancements, Peg was completely cured.

After eight years as a Public Health Service officer, the young psychiatrist saw that the die had been cast: he was going to stay in the Service and he was going to be an administrator. Consequently, on Dr. Kolb's recommendation, he went back to school as a Rockefeller Fellow, taking his master's degree in public health at Johns Hopkins University. It was an important year. It made him one of the first physicians in the country to become schooled both in psychiatry and in public health. And it powerfully nourished ideas that the prevention and treatment of much mental disease, as of much physical disease, required community-wide efforts.

Now World War II was on, and the Service ordered Felix to the Coast Guard Academy at New London, Connecticut, which needed a psychiatrist to help it assess officer candidates. A man who worked with him at the time reports that Felix carried out the assignment admirably, largely because the candidates came to believe that he was not just an interrogator but a person sincerely interested in each individual and his problems. Felix himself is prouder of the fact that as senior medical officer, a post to which he was soon appointed, he was responsible for the physical as well as the emotional health of the thousands of persons at the Academy. He insisted on making calls and serving in the hospital as the other doctors did; he even delivered a few babies.

Even after he became boss of the nation's mental health program, Felix considered himself to be first of all a physician. "If we are ever to break down the walls which have isolated us from the rest of medicine," he told the American Psychiatric Association in his presidential address in 1961, "it must be possible for our nonpsychiatric colleague to expect as much of us vis-à-vis his field as we expect of him in the realm of psychiatry."

Felix generally has three or four patients—troubled souls he has bumped into somewhere, usually at work or at church—each of whom he sees for an hour a week at his home or office. Recent patients have included an alcoholic, a potential suicide, and a woman who could no longer put up with her husband. Felix claims that the best part of his professional day is the time he spends with such people. He feels good for having helped someone, and he is able to mix with clinical colleagues feeling himself not simply a paper-pusher, but their peer.

On the night of Felix's fortieth birthday, when he was feeling a little low because youth had passed, he received a telephone summons from the Public Health Service's chief of personnel to return to Washington and serve a while as assistant chief of the Hospital Division of the Bureau of Medical Services. "Dr. Kolb is retiring," said the personnel chief, "and the Surgeon General wants to keep his eye on you. Either you make good and become chief of the Mental Health Division or go back to the field and know you have had your chance."

When the indicated appointment to Mental Health came through, in November, 1944, it was a matter for some elation since it meant not only a bigger job but also a higher rank: that of medical director, which put him alongside Navy captains and Army colonels. The very next day, nervously making his first appearance at the Capitol to defend an emergency appropriation of $30,000, he tripped over his open brief case and spilled his papers and himself across the committee room floor. He was voted his appropriation—the first in a long series now totaling about three quarters of a billion dollars—out of pity, he thinks.

As new head of the federal government's mental health activities, Felix had several important breaks. For one thing, his predecessor, Dr. Kolb, had been pushing since 1938 for an organization—somewhat like the National Cancer Institute, authorized in 1937—to study mental illness. For another thing, World War II, which had halted Kolb's efforts at a time when the American Medical Association still opposed them, had uncovered an alarming number of emotionally upset people. In good part because of these circumstances, the Mental Health Act of 1946 sailed along with the backing of virtually every interested group.

But there were obstacles ahead, one of them the long and stubbornly held belief that mental illness is an individual matter, not amenable to the public health approach. At lunch one day in the dingy cafeteria of Tempo 6, where Felix's little division was housed, he began talking about prevention. A physician at the table remarked: "I have never seen any proof that mental illness can be prevented." Whereupon Felix pounded the table and said: "But by God I'm going to proceed on that assumption until it's disproved."

"The last twenty years," Felix has been heard to remark in what was probably only a slight overstatement, "have been sweat and blood." Sweat there has been in plenty. To build a staff; to decide where money to tackle such a formless problem as mental illness can be spent most profitably (and, each year, exactly how much); to deal with the competing ideas and requests, inside the Institute and out, of the psychoanalytically oriented school of investigators, who stress unconscious emotional conflicts as the cause of mental disorders, and the biologically oriented investigators, who emphasize the importance of physical processes; and to maintain harmonious relations with organized medicine, the voluntary agencies, Congress, and the budget-minded elements of government—all these endeavors have required intensive and prolonged application, some adeptness at infighting, and great political skill. One observer, less admiring of Felix than most other people who know him, sizes him up as, most of all, an exceedingly adroit juggler. "But I don't know anyone else," he adds, "who could have run this show and kept it on the road."

Some blood has been shed, too, most of it during Felix's determined resistance to what he viewed as efforts to reorganize him out of existence. To Felix, everything connected with the government's mental health program belongs together—can work effectively "only if one person is up there in the control tower."

Some Public Health Service officers considered it logical to take away the NIMH's sizable training program—$49 million in 1963, more than one third of the budget—and merge it with the training programs of the other institutes. The most recent battle over this issue was fought intermittently, with some bitter engagements off-stage, for about a year. Felix ended it by stating that if he were expected to remain as director, there must be no tampering with the Institute.

Felix is a psychiatrist, and, as part of the additional training he took—after office hours—during the early years in Washington, he has been psychoanalyzed; so he understands better than most other people how the mind works and how it can affect the body. Yet, like most of us, he is subject to psychosomatic ills. They generally come on a little after Christmas—a sporadic retinitis, or eye inflammation, and a bothersome stomach—and they die away only after he has gone to the Capitol and defended his appropriations.

In explanation he points out that he has rather weighty responsibilities. About 1,000 persons, ten times as many as at the start, were on the Institute's payroll in 1963; more than a thousand principal researchers in universities and hospitals across the country, and the people working with them, depended upon the Institute at least in part for funds; more than 4,500 persons were receiving NIMH stipends for graduate training; thousands of others owed their livelihood in part to the fact that the Institute contributed to the mental health activities in which they were engaged.

Each year Felix spends weeks reviewing the work of the Institute and its grantees, then the mental health activities of the states, particularly those represented on the congressional committees, and, finally, activities in the rest of the world. Speaking of this homework recently, he was reminded of William Jennings Bryan. "People called him 'the boy orator of the Platte,'" he recalled, "and Bryan's detractors used to say that that was very appropriate because the Platte was a mile wide but only an inch deep. Well, I guess I am that way, too. By the time I have to appear on Capitol Hill, I know a little about a great many subjects, but scratch me very deep and you may draw a blank."

In spite of the trepidation with which Felix approaches "the Hill," he almost invariably comes away with more money than his budget called for. In the ten years ending with 1963, for example, he defended budgets totaling approximately $470 million and was granted additional appropriations of about $120 million. In large part this is because his own budget requests have been modified, first by the National Institutes of Health, then by the Public Health Service, and then by the Bureau of the Budget and the White House. It would be neither ethical nor administratively permissible for Felix to volunteer what his original estimates had been, but if members of Congress ask him, he is permitted to reply; and they do ask.

Occasionally Felix has received more money than he himself asked for or even wanted.

For several years after the tranquilizing drugs were introduced into this country, in 1954, psychiatric opinion about them was widely divided. Felix, along with many other psychiatrists, showed no great enthusiasm for the tranquilizers, but the Institute did some studies and set about preparing, with scientific thoroughness, for a conference that would clarify the research problems and lead to further investigations. The conference was held as scheduled in September, 1956, but Congress, meanwhile, prodded by the National Committee Against Mental Illness, had appropriated $486,000 for work on psychoactive drugs and advised Felix, in effect, to hurry it up. The next year Congress appropriated $2 million.

Because the tranquilizing drugs have turned out to be the most dramatic single discovery in the history of mental illness, some authorities outside the Institute believe that the episode demonstrated on Felix's part a lack of initiative and foresight. Felix comments merely that he was not so enthusiastic about the drugs as he might have been, and as he is now.

Some thirty-five or forty psychoactive drugs—both tranquilizers and antidepressives—had become available for prescription use by 1963, and pharmaceutical houses here and abroad were racing to put together new ones. During 1962 and 1963, NIMH grantees tested some 150 experimental drugs and found none of them superior to those already available; several of the new ones, though, may be marketed.

The Institute received another windfall when Congress, hearkening again to influential individuals and agencies outside the government, voted money for the psychiatric training of general practitioners and other doctors who are not psychiatrists. One provision, enabling doctors already in practice to go back and take three-year full-time residencies in psychiatry, Felix had opposed on the ground that the country needed these doctors where they were. Four years after the program opened in 1959, several hundred physicians had given up their old fields and, on annual stipends running to $12,000, were in the process of becoming psychiatrists. Felix still didn't like the idea. He was happy, however, about a provision under which several thousand doctors were studying psychiatry on a part-time basis, for he has long held that the family physician should be capable of diagnosing mental ailments and treating many patients himself, referring the others to a psychiatrist. In support, Felix cites the finding of the Joint Commission on Mental Illness and Health: that clergymen first, and then family doctors, not psychiatrists, are the ones most often consulted by persons with emotional problems.

The Joint Commission made the first comprehensive study in history of this country's mental health needs and resources and reported in 1961. During the hearings of the Cabinet-level committee appointed by President Kennedy to review the report and make recommendations, Felix succeeded in getting across his view that the report should have placed more emphasis on community health centers.

Felix shares the widespread belief that eventually mental illness will be found to have a physical basis. "We know that people are born with different abilities to react to stress," he explains. "Some can adapt to almost any amount of it; others go to pieces quickly. Genetics has a chemical basis, so at least part of the trouble must be chemical. Presumably a person who reaches his breaking point abnormally early has a metabolic abnormality—like the diabetic or the child with phenylketonuria. Hopefully some day we shall be able to give that person something so that he will respond to stress much the same as other persons. Maybe we can go one step further: maybe we shall be able chemically to reverse the process."

Meanwhile, he emphasizes, mental illness has strong sociological and psychological, as well as biological, components, and what we know about those we have to put to work. Meanwhile, too, since the causes of most forms of mental illness remain unknown, he continues to encourage research ranging from how an individual brain cell operates to how people get along in groups. Much of this takes place in the part of the NIH clinical center at Bethesda, Maryland, allotted to Felix's Institute. There, at any one time, NIMH scientists have a variety of groups under observation—for example:

. A number of schizophrenic persons whose families come in regularly to participate in the newest treatment of mental illness—family therapy, in which all members air opinions and ask questions. (When schizophrenia develops in a young person, it now appears that a significant factor has been the relationship of the family as a whole, not just the often emphasized relationship between mother and child.)

. An entire family, parents and three children, one of them schizophrenic.

. A dozen college students who have had emotional breakdowns.

. A group of persons suffering from depression.

An important part of the Institute's research is sparked by a special unit of sociologists, psychologists, and psychiatrists—formed and fostered by Felix and having offices just down the hall from his—known as the Professional Services Branch. The unit serves as a privy council to decide what mental health problems need more attention and to plan exploratory work.

Among the pioneering projects that have paid off most handsomely was a study on the rehabilitation of the mentally ill. On certain floors of the Boston State Hospital, patients continued to be treated as usual; on the other floors, additional rehabilitation people were hired—recreational therapists, occupational therapists, and social service workers—and the patients on those floors were able to leave the hospital sooner. Thanks to this and related projects, rehabilitation programs among mental hospital patients and former patients have become relatively common, many of them financed through the Institute's Research Utilization Branch. The special planning unit also promoted some of the earliest work on mental retardation, suicide, and aging, and recently sponsored studies on alcoholism, including a nationwide survey of drinking habits.

Concerned also with what fosters mental *health,* the Institute began systematically to study the factors influencing human beings from infancy to adulthood. Several years ago doctors and psychologists crossed Wisconsin Avenue to the United States Naval Hospital and, over a period of months, examined about a hundred newborn babies. Then they studied the attitudes, expectations, and personalities of their parents. (Even brand-new babies differ: some from the very start want a special amount of cuddling, while others display more vigor and independence; and there may be trouble if a family that wanted a vigorous child gets a cuddly one instead.) The Institute has set up its own nursery school for these children and hopes to follow them through the years. Meanwhile other research teams are studying the successful adolescent in contrast to the adolescent who has broken down.

*

Dr. and Mrs. Felix live with their daughter, Kathy, in a commodious, white-painted brick rambler only a few minutes' drive from the NIH campus. The basement contains the doctor's woodworking shop and a recreation room, featuring a bar over which is displayed the warning: "Alcohol Makes People See Double and Act Single." Neither of the Felixes drinks much. In view of his wide interests—which include reading history and biography, as well as photography, theater, good music, and driving to Colorado—it might be thought that Felix would look toward retirement with some pleasure. "But the woodworking, the picture taking, all those things," he protested recently, "—those are all things I do for myself. And I have to be helping others, or die."

He said this without attitudinizing and as if it were common knowledge.

Felix spends most of his working hours in conference. Like Washington dentists, he is dated days in advance—for consultations with staff members, Public Health Service officials, members of Congress, state officials, and a variety of other people, in and out of government, interested in mental illness. He is too busy for daily dictation; letters that cannot be handled by his staff accumulate until, once a week or so, he makes time for a two- or three-hour session with a secretary. Yet fellow workers who need a word with the boss can usually get it.

When the pressure becomes too great, he strolls down the hall, tells a joke or two—generally naughty—and kids the girls, calling them endearing names and saying how wonderful they look.

In his frequent talks to medical students and psychiatric residents, Felix is apt to discuss a psychiatric case in great clinical detail and then throw out some hard questions: "What does this person have to go back to? What should be happening in the community to reduce the number of such cases? What about people who make $5,000 a year— can *they* pay $20 an hour five days a week if somebody in the family gets mentally ill? What are you going to do?"

Felix *hopes* that they—and the people in his other audiences—will work for the establishment of community centers that will diagnose mental illness early and treat it right there in the community.

Not every psychiatrist was convinced that the program for community-centered mental health facilities would work as well as President Kennedy and Felix envisaged. Some wondered whether the public was as yet well enough informed to accept the idea of mental patients' remaining in the midst of the community. They wondered, too, whether, once the community centers were well established, the state mental hospitals could discharge as many patients as the supporters of the new program anticipated. But Felix's enthusiasm for the program and his conviction that it would open a new era in the prevention and treatment of mental illness were so great that he told a group of colleagues, with customary gusto: "Boys, I'm too old to get anything out of this myself. Boys, you can ride with me, or you can get off and walk."

The birth of the program coincided with Felix's thirtieth anniversary in the Public Health Service. At this point, he was eligible to retire on 75 per cent of his base pay and accept one of several offers of jobs paying twice as much as he then received—roughly $20,000, counting allowances. "It's always great," he said, "to know that somebody wants you." But he was also heard to remark that, as Director of NIMH at this great moment in the history of the campaign against mental illness, he was beginning to feel like Moses looking into the Promised Land.

Robert M. Ball

HE HAS YOUR NUMBER

OSCAR SCHISGALL

THE TRUSTEES OF
PRINCETON UNIVERSITY

BY VIRTUE OF THE AUTHORITY VESTED IN THEM

UNDER A PROGRAM INITIATED BY JOHN D. ROCKEFELLER 3RD

TO STRENGTHEN THE CAREER

SERVICE IN THE FEDERAL GOVERNMENT

DO HEREBY GRANT A

ROCKEFELLER PUBLIC SERVICE AWARD

TO

ROBERT M. BALL

IN RECOGNITION OF DISTINGUISHED SERVICE

TO THE GOVERNMENT OF THE UNITED STATES

AND TO THE AMERICAN PEOPLE

PRESIDENT

CLERK

DONE IN NASSAU HALL
PRINCETON, NEW JERSEY

ROBERT M. BALL

Not every human adventure occurs on battlefields or in spacecraft or on the rolling deck of a Spanish galleon. Some of the greatest exploits in mankind's history were those of quiet men who sat still and allowed their imaginations to soar. Theirs were adventures of mind and spirit.

Robert M. Ball, Commissioner of Social Security, has made his place among those who served with ideas. Yet he calls his twenty years of quiet public service "a time of adventure and excitement."

He was a young man of twenty-seven—tall, dark-haired, earnest—when he came to work in the Bureau of Old Age and Survivors Insurance in 1939. The government agency was only three years old at the time; later it became part of the Social Security Administration. Though Wesleyan University had given him an B.A. degree in 1935 and an M.A. in economics in 1936 (plus election to Phi Beta

Kappa), Ball began his government service as a lowly CAF-3. Considering his college degrees, it was about as humble a rank as the Civil Service could offer. Nevertheless, as he now points out, it was probably the best thing that could have happened.

For he became a field assistant attached to the Newark, New Jersey, field office. In that assignment he had to confer with hundreds of bewildered people who were trying to discover how they fitted into the new concept of social security.

Though he had been given a period of indoctrination, Ball soon discovered that some of the people he saw were asking questions that were not easy to answer. The questioners were, for instance, the early beneficiaries of the system. They were receiving only $22 per month on the average. Surely they could not live on that. What, they wanted to know, was the government expecting them to do?

Then there were the employers, often exasperated, who were being asked to fill out new forms and to assume new responsibilities. A few simply could not understand what was expected of them. It was up to field representatives like Ball to clarify duties, to pacify irritated opponents of the plan, to persuade them that this was no "New Deal madness."

"I think I learned more about social security in those days of working at the grass roots," he says, "than I could have learned in any other way."

But the most significant thing he learned—a lesson that has animated his entire career—was this:

The Bureau of Old Age and Survivors Insurance

(BOASI) dealt with human needs and emotions. The people Ball met when he was a field assistant were in large number elderly, anxious citizens with uncertain futures, and widows and orphans recently bereaved. Many of them looked to the years ahead with fear.

From the start Ball recognized his job as one of providing not only material aid but also reassurance to multitudes of Americans who had never known anything like this before.

At that time the social security program faced the opposition of many skeptics and deriders. Some of its opponents called the entire social security idea impractical. They called it socialistic. They called it contrary to the American principle of self-reliance. "Let a thing like this catch hold," they were saying, "and we're on the road to a welfare state."

This kind of opposition disturbed but did not dishearten those who were getting the new program started. On the contrary, the early years of social security constituted a period in which its organizers' confidence ran high. Every employee knew he was part of a vigorous new development on the American scene. Even the most menial job became an important pioneering step in a sociological adventure destined to transform the future of the nation.

"In those early years," Ball says, "those of us who were the rank and file of the Bureau could only marvel at the fine organizational and developmental work of those, both inside and outside of government, who set the program up. Among those to be credited with shaping OASI were Professor Edwin Witte, who headed the staff of the Committee on Economic Security which drafted the legislation, and Arthur J. Altmeyer, who became Chairman of the Social Security Board and later Commissioner of Social Security. And there was Wilbur J. Cohen, adviser to both Witte and Altmeyer, who by 1963 was Assistant Secretary of Health, Education and Welfare. There were John Winant, former Governor of New Hampshire and the first Chairman of the Social Security Board, and John Corson, who, as Director of the Bureau of Old Age and Survivors Insurance, did so much to get the program started properly. There were many, many more like them, and those of us who were young in the Bureau looked upon them all as great trail blazers—which, of course, they were."

Perhaps the best way to understand the significance of Robert Ball's praise of early planning is to appraise a few of its results. When he went to work for the Bureau, the social security program covered some 34 million workers in commerce and industry. During 1963, 76 million workers and self-employed people in a wide variety of fields had earnings credited for social security purposes.

The machinery for keeping the individual wage record accounts was set up in 1939, but the organization was just getting ready to provide monthly benefits for the first time.

By 1963 more than 18 million people were receiving social security benefits every month—not just retired workers but also the wives of such workers, aged widows, dependent parents, orphaned children and their mothers, disabled men and their wives and children.

Through the Social Security Administration, in addition to retirement and disability protection, Americans have the equivalent of over $500 billion of life insurance in force.

Robert Ball, having come up through the ranks, heads an administration with a working force of 37,000. The modern home office of the Social Security Administration in Baltimore, Maryland, is one of the largest government installations in the nation. Its myriad records are handled by one of the largest assemblages of electronic computers and magnetic tape files anywhere on earth. (This is logical because no other insurance system has ever matched the size of social security in America.)

The remarkable thing about this explosive growth, from a small bureau to an institution affecting the lives of practically all living Americans, is that it occurred within the space of twenty-five years—that is, within the working years of many of its early employees, like Ball.

There is a curious paradox in his public service career: as he himself puts it, he once served the social security program best by leaving it.

That was in 1945. The American Council on Education, foreseeing the future needs of an institution like social security, created a Committee on Education and Social Security. The purpose was to develop training and educational opportunities for people who were making careers in this new field.

By then Ball had, of course, risen quite a way from the first Newark job. He had at various times been an assistant manager and a manager of other district offices. In Baltimore, meanwhile, the central office of the Bureau, as well as the field organization, had been growing fast. The budget and personnel had been expanded to take care of the millions of Americans who were every year being added to the social security roster.

The Bureau constantly had to train new people to cope with these demands of growth. The best way to train them was to let them share the experience of veteran workers. So Ball had been brought in from the field to become an instructor. In Baltimore and in field offices he lectured, explained, trained, and analyzed cases for newly hired personnel.

In view of Ball's experience in training others, the Director of the newly formed Committee on Education and Social Security, Karl de Schweinitz, saw in him the kind of man needed to help shape the Committee's program. He was offered the job and took it, as Assistant Director. But actually, though no longer on Social Security's staff, Ball was still serving the program. He was training others to work for social security.

Two years later, in 1947, the United States Senate decided to have a close look at social security. It created an advisory council whose function would be to study the social security program and to make legislative recommendations for its future.

Its membership included former Secretary of State Edward R. Stettinius, Jr.; economist Sumner H. Slichter of Harvard; J. Douglas Brown, Dean of the Faculty at Princeton; Marion B. Folsom, who later became Secretary of Health, Education and Welfare; Emil Rieve, president of the Textile Workers' Union and vice-president of the CIO; Nelson Cruikshank of the AFL, and others of equal distinction.

Almost the first thing this advisory council needed was a

staff director who knew social security so thoroughly that he could guide the council in its studies. Members of the council began to look around; in Ball they saw a man whose background and experience fitted him perfectly to become the council's staff director.

"I'd had nine years of experience with Social Security and I believed in it with all my heart," Ball said. "I saw this program as making a major contribution to the solution of the problem of poverty in the United States. Its emphasis upon self-help, with rights based upon work and contributions, was very important to me. I considered social insurance to be a practical method of accomplishing a great social goal in a way that protected the freedom of the individual. I could think of no better way to serve this cause than to work with the Senate Advisory Council."

By this time Ball was in his thirties. He was married; he had a son. He was enjoying his job. He discussed the change in career with Doris, his wife, then accepted the new post. Many of his associates maintain that his joining the council was the best thing that could have happened for American social security.

Not that he permitted his personal enthusiasm to affect the council's impartial approach to the investigation. Even those of its members who had doubts about the program later agreed that Ball's work had been scrupulously thorough and objective.

What his presence at the council table accomplished was to guarantee that the body would know every facet of every social security problem; that it would consider details it might easily have overlooked. While he worked as the council's staff director—during 1948 and 1949—Ball made one thing clear to everybody: he himself had a great storehouse of knowledge about social security.

By this time—1949—about 60 per cent of America's employed people were covered by the old age and death benefits that social security offered. About two and a half million people were receiving checks that totaled slightly more than $56 million per month. (By way of contrast, it should be noted that in 1963 the more than 18 million recipients of benefits shared a monthly disbursement of almost $1 1/2 billion.)

When Ball sat down to give the council a summary of all that had happened in the first thirteen years of the social security program, he faced a bewildering challenge. How could you present to the council the full size of the job that had been accomplished and of the job that still needed to be done?

Foremost among the problems that faced the program was the lag in benefits behind the rising economy of the war and postwar periods. Benefits were still geared to the low earnings of the late 1930's. The average old age insurance benefit for people on the rolls in December, 1948, for example, was just a little over $25 a month.

If social insurance was to keep congressional and public support and not be replaced by some general pension scheme paid from the general treasury, the benefit scale would have to be increased very substantially.

Then, too, it would not suffice to increase the benefits while so many people were still not covered by the program. The Congress, at the start, had included only wage workers in commerce and industry—not because agricultural and domestic workers or self-employed persons had less need for the program, but because the job of including these vast groups seemed too difficult for a new organization to tackle.

Ball remembered the days when critics of the program said you simply could not enroll America's heterogeneous working population in a single record-keeping system. You could not keep track of their earnings for social security purposes. You could not monitor every small firm or self-employed person in the United States to make sure there was compliance with regulations. Administering such a venture would be beyond all hope.

Social security, it had been prophesied, must eventually collapse because of its own unwieldy weight. It would, moreover, lead to the most monstrous confusion of records this country had ever known.

"Damn it, man," one critical friend had said to Ball, "we'll have to set half the nation's people to keeping accounts of what the other half does!"

But Ball recalled also that in Baltimore and in the many field offices everybody—"and I mean at every level," he insists, "from top echelons to lowest"—was constantly seeking ways of improving and accelerating the agency's work. No doubt one of the greatest of all its blessings was the rapid development of punch-card machines and later of electronic data processing equipment. Without them, and without the foresight of capable men like Joseph L. Fay who were in charge of setting up the mechanical operations, the agency might well have become paralyzed.

Ball says: "Whenever a new machine came in, a group would stand around it in awe. They realized that many of them had shared in telling the inventors and manufacturers what they wanted these machines to do. They had initiated the thinking of the designers by telling them their problems. And so when these social security workers saw such problems mechanically solved, they knew they'd had a personal part in the creation of these machines."

In any case, Ball was able to tell the Senate Advisory Council, out of his personal experience, how efficient mechanical office procedures had been developed to keep pace with the explosive growth of the files. What had seemed an impossible task a few years earlier was actually being done.

From the start Ball himself had been one of the most ardent supporters of the theory that social security ought to apply to *all* working Americans. At one point in his career with the Bureau of Old Age and Survivors Insurance, he had been in charge of planning ways to extend coverage. But was it really feasible?

It had been a formidable enough job to enroll those who worked in firms that remained in the same location and kept careful records. How could you possibly obtain similar records for wandering farm workers? For household help? For self-employed people—say, plumbers, retailers, artists, small farmers, and many more categories? In other words, how could social security be expanded to meet the needs of all people?

"The job is too big to be practicable," some said. Ball heard those words many times. Yet he and other social security people felt certain that, with the public's cooperation, it could be done.

So, in spite of the difficulties that might lie ahead, Ball was gratified when the Senate Advisory Council recommended broadening the scope of social security to include: self-employed farmers, business and professional people; farm workers; employees of nonprofit institutions; household workers; federal civilian employees; railroad employees; members of the Armed Forces; and employees of state and local governments.

"None of these enjoyed the privileges of social security at the time," Ball said. "It seemed tragic that large groups of working people whose need for security was just as great as those covered should be left out of the program, primarily for administrative reasons."

But, just as important, Ball—and many other people in Social Security—wanted something more. They wanted disability insurance for all workers: payments made to those who, through accident or a collapse of health, were left permanently unable to support themselves and their families.

"We felt," Ball said, "that if the breadwinner of a family could no longer earn any wages—through disability—his family's finances suffered as grievously as if he were dead. In fact, the family faced expenses that would not have existed in cases of the breadwinner's death: medical treatment for the invalid, for one thing, plus food for him, clothing, housing, and so on. To be realistic, Social Security would have to recognize the fact that total disability terminates one's income as sharply as does death or retirement."

Again the skeptics were heard: "Who's going to decide if a man is incapable of earning a living? If he dies, that's conclusive. There's no question about the needs of his widow and children. But as long as he's alive, the problem of whether he can earn some money or not becomes a matter of somebody's judgment. Whose judgment?"

Another objection to adding disability to the social security benefits was that such protection might deter rehabilitation. Some said once a person was put on the benefit rolls, he would not be interested in going back to work. But those who pointed out the great economic hardships resulting from the permanent and total disability of wage earners were insistent that disability could be proved. They were sure the administrative obstacles could be overcome. Ball was among those who insisted that disability protection under social insurance was practicable.

The council deliberated for months. Ball regards the results of this council as one of the milestones of social security—and working with it, one of the most rewarding experiences of his life. For the group endorsed the principles of the social security system as it existed, praised its manner of operation, and recommended plans for increasing benefit levels, expanding the coverage, and adopting the disability insurance in which Ball so earnestly believed.

It was now 1949, and in that year the Social Security Administration rehired Ball and made him Assistant Director—later Deputy Director—of the OASI Bureau. He now had a key role in developing the administration's legislative proposals. He also served as a source of information to Congress in its consideration of changes in the social security program.

The first of these changes, recommended by the Senate Advisory Council, were the 1950 social security amendments. These raised social security benefits substantially (benefits of people already on the rolls were doubled, on the average). They raised the yearly amount of earnings that were subject to social security contributions and could be used for figuring benefits; and they extended social security protection to many self-employed people: agricultural and domestic workers, employees of nonprofit organizations, public employees, and others.

Then came the 1952 election, which brought more changes and a new challenge.

Simultaneously there were, first, a new national administration; second, an increased status for social security with the establishment of the Department of Health, Education and Welfare; and third, an influx into the top jobs of the new Department of people who had had no experience with social security.

Ball's past as a training instructor now stood him in good stead. He had to orient the top staff of the new Department in the entire social security program.

When a group of outside consultants on social security was established by the Eisenhower administration, Ball acted as its staff director. These consultants, after making a thorough study of the program, recommended still further extensions of coverage.

But one of the most notable legislative improvements in social security was still to come. A bill setting up a disability insurance program under Social Security was passed by the House for the second time late in 1955. Now this important new program faced a rocky road in the Senate.

The measure was vigorously opposed by insurance groups, medical societies, and spokesmen for the Eisenhower administration. When the bill was considered by the Senate Finance Committee in 1956, the disability program was not approved. The only hope for the legislation was that the proposal could be restored through a fight on the floor of the Senate.

Nobody could predict which way the Senate's vote would go. If the bill lost, a vital segment of social security would be lost or delayed.

Senator Walter George of Georgia rose to make a speech. It started quietly; it gained momentum. Before it was half finished most of the senators knew they were listening to a masterpiece. Senator George extolled and dramatized the humanitarian principles of social security. Not long after the speech ended, the vote was taken and the disability insurance proposal won by the margin of a single vote.

The closeness of this vote was reflected in the conservative character of the disability program that was approved in 1956. The measure provided social security benefits for permanently and totally disabled workers only after they had reached the age of fifty. Moreover, the disability must have lasted through six months before benefits could begin. No benefits were provided for wives and children of disabled workers.

In 1958 these family benefits were added, however, and in 1960 the age-fifty limit was removed. Thus the new—and, at first, highly controversial—disability program won wide acceptance as an important part of the social security system.

The successive social security amendments of the 1950's launched a new epoch not only for social security but for Robert M. Ball. It was an epoch in which he was able to say in a speech to his agency's district managers: "Today it can be taken for granted that the abolition of want in the United States is no longer a problem of economic capacity. It is solely a problem of our willingness to organize to do the job." Not that he believed social security alone could abolish poverty, but that in a dynamic economy it would make a big contribution to reaching this goal.

The expansion of coverage to all kinds of working groups caused an explosion in the number of names in the social security files. They include well over 90 per cent of all American wage earners. More people in the United States enjoy a system of social security protection, a system created by democratic procedures, than in any other country.

Yet the efficiency of the agency usually amazes visitors to the Baltimore headquarters. One such caller asked Mrs. Leona V. MacKinnon, Ball's assistant, how long it would take a citizen to learn what his social security number was if he lost his card.

"Let's time it," Mrs. MacKinnon suggested. She led the visitor to the proper department. He gave his name and date of birth to a supervisor. The supervisor put the information into code and repeated the code over the telephone. The correct social security number was placed on the supervisor's desk within forty seconds!

In spite of its complexities, administering the entire program costs only two cents out of every dollar contributed—leaving ninety-eight cents for benefits. This is a record that could well be envied by any private insurance company.

When one has taken a big bite, there must always be a period for chewing, swallowing, digesting. Each time the scope of social security was broadened, the agency had to find ways of handling its new responsibilities.

So its personnel plunged into successive periods of hard work done quietly, in conferences and on drawing boards, in Baltimore and Washington and in hundreds of field offices. New machinery and new methods had to be made to function smoothly. The American people had to be informed of their new rights and privileges, of their new duties as participants in social security.

For Ball, these intervals became some of the busiest periods of his life. They were years of tremendous growth for the organization. Many thousands of new employees had to be trained to meet Social Security's added responsibilities. The number of district offices had to be increased month after month; they had to be established close to the millions of people who streamed to them for assistance and for information. (Today there are more than 600 such district offices throughout the United States.)

During these years of growth of the agency, Ball was elevated to high posts in various professional organizations. He became, for example, Vice-President of the American Public Welfare Association, and a member of the Executive Committee of the National Council on the Aging. He became a member of the committee of social insurance experts of the International Labor Organization and a member of the governing board of the International Social Security Association.

And also, as an outstanding event of the "developing" years, the Department of Health, Education and Welfare gave him its Distinguished Service Award. This was the first year, 1954, in which such awards were bestowed.

Ball was among those immediately chosen for the certifi-
cate, which now decorates his office wall. But it is not
alone. Beside it hangs the Career Service Award of the
National Civil Service League, given to him in 1958.
There are two or three others; and climactically, his most
recent honor, the Rockefeller Public Service Award.

Obviously, the years were eventful. For one thing, there
were the investigations.

"Just after the Eisenhower administration came into
office and while the newly appointed consultants were
studying the program," Ball recalls, "the Committee on
Ways and Means of the House established a subcommittee under Representative [later Senator] Carl Curtis of
Nebraska to investigate the social security program. This
investigation was a searching and detailed inquiry, not
only into our administrative practices and policies but
also into the fundamental principles of social security."

Ball answered detailed questions about the program
for days on end.

"We were constantly being studied by various groups,"
he says. In 1957 the Secretary of Health, Education and
Welfare appointed a committee of outstanding businessmen, with Reinhard Hohaus, vice-president of the Met-
ropolitan Life Insurance Company as chairman, to look
into the administration of the Bureau of Old Age and
Survivors Insurance. After a year of study, their major
finding was: ". . . the consultants believe that the Bureau
is carrying out its mission in a sound and vigorous manner. It should be a source of satisfaction to the Secretary to
know that the Bureau has been a pioneer in the very
difficult matter of introducing automatic machinery into

the paperwork area with substantial savings to the trust funds. . . . The consultants were impressed with the effective and competent manner in which the staff of the Bureau appeared to be managing their responsibilities . . . with the way the Bureau personnel met and dealt with the public and with the impression of both efficiency and friendliness created by the typical OASI district office."

By the time the next congressional inquiry into the program came around, Ball was in his forties, the father of two children, Jonathan and Jacqueline. Also, he had become a seasoned public servant.

This congressional examination of the social security program concerned the disability provisions. It was made in 1959 by a subcommittee of the Ways and Means Committee of the House headed by Representative Burr P. Harrison of Virginia. Congressman Harrison and his colleagues were determined to make a careful and penetrating investigation. They were not at all satisfied with what they knew about the program.

Under Ball's direction, reports were drafted, charts were prepared, and statistics assembled. Every bit of relevant information about the administration of the disability program was made available to the committee. Those who were present at the initial hearings still recall Ball's explanatory statement to the committee as a model of clarity. Day after day Robert Ball, Victor Christgau, Director of the Bureau of Old Age and Survivors Insurance, Arthur Hess (later Director of the Division of Disability Operations) and others faced the investigating committee. They answered questions fully, patiently, with reference to the previously prepared charts. They listened to the testimony of countless other witnesses. This went on for months.

What had begun as an investigation by people who expected to find serious evidence of mismanagement slowly changed its tone. The thoroughness and candor with which the Social Security officials presented the facts won more and more respect. Before the inquiry ended the committee had changed its attitude. Congressman Harrison publicly said to the agency's representatives: "We did not understand the vastness of this program and the facts of its rapid and great growth. We have some appreciation now, some little realization, which I know we did not have when we started this inquiry, of what a tremendous task the Congress had imposed on you and the diligence and intelligence with which your Bureau and its officials have gone about in trying to carry it out. . . . The fact that I have disagreed individually, or other members of the committee have disagreed on some of the details of this enormous program, should not be considered as to detract in any way from our conviction that on the whole the program has been administered very fairly and with great capacity by excellent public officials. . . .

"We are particularly grateful to Mr. Ball, who has demonstrated his great capacity and his dedication to performance of these services with his great ability."

When a formerly skeptical congressman makes a statement like that, a public servant knows he has done his job well. Ball undoubtedly treasures Congressman Harrison's words as much as he prizes the awards that hang on his office wall.

The Commissioner's long service in Social Security has

truly been a time of exciting adventure—the adventure of growth, of expansion, of enacting new ideas. It is significant that almost every time there has been an examination of the program (and there have been many) the results have been to endorse the work of the Social Security Administration and to approve plans for expansion of the program.

In Ball's opinion, the adventure is just beginning. Social security in America, less than thirty years old, is still in its first management generation. Viewed in the long perspective of history, it is an infant. But it is an infant that has developed extraordinary vigor and efficiency.

One reason for this continued efficiency is that a trained and experienced top staff have kept moving together toward a set of common objectives. In 1958 Ball undertook to state these objectives carefully and in permanent form. He produced a "Statement of Bureau Objectives," meant as a guidepost for employees of the organization. The booklet prompted Arthur Flemming, when Secretary of Health, Education and Welfare, to declare: "This is the finest statement of its kind by a government agency that it has been my privilege to read."

The strength of the statement lay in its simplicity. It began by listing four points of the Bureau's own responsibilities—which, incidentally, were four pillars of Ball's personal philosophy:

(1) *To the public:* To safeguard and ensure the rights of the public under the program, to provide the full measure of service to which the public is entitled, and to promote economical administration.

(2) *For the program:* To improve the program so that

it will more completely achieve its purpose and play its optimum role in providing economic security to the nation's workers and their families.

(3) *To the government as a whole:* For the contributions we can make to government-wide policy and programs.

(4) *To the employees of the Bureau:* For the establishment and maintenance of an administrative climate and working conditions that will foster an effective career service.

The booklet went on to outline, in clear, forthright terms, specific objectives under each responsibility. For example, under responsibility to the public: "Treat everyone who comes to an OASI office or gets a letter or other communication from any part of the Bureau as deserving of respect and entitled to courteous, friendly, helpful service. OASI is the translation into operations of the spirit and objectives of contributory social insurance. The way the OASI program is administered determines almost as much as the statute itself what the concept of right means in practice. We are, of course, firm about requirements and must sometimes take actions contrary to what our 'customers' want, but our goal under all circumstances is to carry out the program in a way that is friendly, courteous, and humane." The concluding paragraph eloquently expressed the philosophy of the Civil Service:

"The business of the United States is the most important, challenging, and exciting business in the world and we must be able to attract to it the best minds and skill of the next generation. We who are in government owe it to the country to set an example of government business that will compare favorably with the very best in private industry."

"You will find that our staff is quite proud of its efficiency," Ball has told interviewers. He is right. People who file claims for old age or survivors' benefits have discovered that they generally receive their first payment checks within a month to six weeks. Thereafter the payments arrive with undeviating promptness every month.

This waiting interval is not long when one considers what has to be accomplished within those weeks: Local offices assist the applicant in assembling the various proofs (such as proof of age and relationship); the wage record must be examined and benefit rates computed; and the benefit amounts certified to the Treasury Department for payment.

But one thing must here be said—and Robert Ball says it as emphatically as every man who works with him: Every effort is made to avoid real hardship. Payments are sometimes rushed through in as little as two weeks.

This happens in the case of community disasters. The Texas City explosions of a few years ago were an example. Hundreds lost their lives. The entire community was plunged into agony and hardship. The families of the workers who were killed needed income at once. The Social Security Administration immediately revved up its motors, so to speak. In record time it rushed in its financial support in the form of monthly benefits to eligible survivors. This has been true in other disaster areas, too.

As would be expected, disability claims processing is not as fast as the processing of old age or survivors' claims. Proving that a person has had his sixty-fifth birthday or that family relationships exist, for example, is not as complicated, nor does it take as long as getting medical evidence that a person is disabled. The law also requires that most disability cases be sent to a state agency for a disability determination, and then the case must be reviewed by the Social Security Administration because it is federal money that will be used to pay the benefits. All of this takes time. One of Ball's special concerns is that his staff continually look for every possible way to cut down on the time.

In April of 1962, Ball left the career civil service to become Commissioner of Social Security, a Presidential appointment. He had been the top career employee of the Bureau of Old Age and Survivors Insurance since 1952, when he was made Deputy Director at the age of thirty-eight.

Responsible to the Secretary of Health, Education and Welfare for both administration and policy, he is engaged in plans for the future.

What area of human needs will social security embrace next?

Before the Congress, in 1963, was the proposal to bring under social security elderly citizens who could no longer afford today's high hospital costs. The plan was the center of bitter controversy. Among its most articulate opponents was the American Medical Association. Ball was not disheartened by this opposition.

"Every group has the right—in fact, the obligation—to state its opinion," he said. "I expect this legislation to pass. And this I know from past experience: though the A.M.A. opposed disability payments almost as bitterly as they now oppose medical care, once the law was passed the A.M.A. cooperated with us wholeheartedly. They did everything they could, with counsel and assistance, to make disability insurance work. I am confident that if hospital insurance becomes the law, the A.M.A., as the organization of a highly respected profession, will take the same attitude of cooperation."

Meanwhile, as Commissioner of Social Security, he is Chairman of a new Advisory Council on Social Security established by law. This council, the first since the 1948 council to examine all aspects of the program, will make its recommendations for legislative changes by the end of 1964. "Social security can be made into a much more effective weapon than it is today in the battle against poverty and insecurity," the Commissioner says. "There are still many improvements to be made."

When we realize that more than 90 million Americans are insured under social security so that they and their dependents have protection under the program; when we realize that over the years the amounts sent out to elderly citizens, widows, orphans, and the disabled have steadily increased, so that today the monthly maximum is about $127 for the man of the family, about $63 more for his wife, and a maximum of $254 for families with children; when we realize that all this has been accomplished in less than three decades; and when we realize how big a contribution has been made to this social advance by a small group of dedicated civil servants of whom Robert M. Ball is now Commissioner—then we can indeed take pride in those quiet adventurers who sit at their desks and help chart the course of humanity's progress.

Richard E. McArdle

GUARDIAN OF THE BIG TREES

MILTON MACKAYE

THE TRUSTEES OF
PRINCETON UNIVERSITY

BY VIRTUE OF THE AUTHORITY VESTED IN THEM

UNDER A PROGRAM INITIATED BY JOHN D. ROCKEFELLER 3RD

TO STRENGTHEN THE CAREER

SERVICE IN THE FEDERAL GOVERNMENT

DO HEREBY GRANT A

ROCKEFELLER PUBLIC SERVICE AWARD

TO

RICHARD E. McARDLE

IN RECOGNITION OF DISTINGUISHED SERVICE

TO THE GOVERNMENT OF THE UNITED STATES

AND TO THE AMERICAN PEOPLE

PRESIDENT

CLERK

DONE IN NASSAU HALL
PRINCETON, NEW JERSEY

RICHARD E. MC ARDLE

Paris in the autumn of 1918 seemed a long way from home
to a good many young American soldiers. One of them was
Richard E. McArdle, raised in Virginia, who was later to
become Chief of the United States Forest Service. Through
the blind drawings of the military lottery, this ruddy-faced
young man found himself transferred from his engineering
company to a motor pool in France's capital—and driving
the beflagged, official car of Colonel E. M. House, President Wilson's emissary in Europe.

This was not onerous work, and McArdle enjoyed his
anonymous but real proximity to the great and near great.
When Colonel House entertained at his mansion at 88, rue
de l'Université, naval enlisted men served as footmen and
ushers, and McArdle was usually on hand to help them. It
was a big day in his life when Marshal Foch, the Allied
commander in chief, Premier Clemenceau of France,

Prime Minister Lloyd George of Britain, and half a dozen others come to call.

Their conference with Colonel House was prolonged and time hung heavy on McArdle's hands. On a long table were the coats and hats of the eminent visitors, and an errant curiosity took possession of the lighthearted boy from Norfolk: he wondered how he would look in Marshal Foch's military cap. A moment later he stood before a mirror; Foch's sweat-stained kepi slid down to his ears. Lloyd George's fedora, he discovered, was a better fit. A moment later several junior naval officers entered the room and joined joyously in the hat game. A camera was produced and the Clemenceau and Lloyd George derbies, the Foch kepi, went with them into the cobbled courtyard where they snapped one another's pictures.

A sharp whistle put an abrupt end to laughter. "They're coming!" said a scared voice from the door. In a moment the young officers had scuttled to the stables and McArdle stood alone in the courtyard with the chapeaus of the mighty guiltily in his hands. Stiff-legged, he moved into the reception room.

"Where in the hell is my hat?" he heard Clemenceau say in English. And then, to his surprise and relief, he heard himself say: "Forgive me, Your Excellencies. I did not want these hats to be crushed by your overcoats and took them into another room." Today he is not quite sure whether it was with guilt or triumph that he bowed out three of the most famous men in the world.

There was another big day in Paris for McArdle, a day that discovered to him his life career. It was six or seven months after the end of the war, but he was still in military service, a sergeant now, and back in Paris on furlough. In the center of the city the American Library Association maintained a stall where United States troops could borrow books. There weren't many books, but McArdle went in to borrow. When he left the place he carried with him *Elements of Forestry,* by Moon and Brown, and *First Book of Forestry.* McArdle hardly knew the horse chestnuts of the Paris avenues from the willows along the Seine, and he had never heard of forestry as a profession; but when he finished reading those (to him) exciting volumes he knew what he was meant to be. It was an almost instant conversion, and it was a lasting one.

As a long-time reporter I have talked to many distinguished men about their beginnings and have never known one who had so few early doubts as Dick McArdle. When he came home from military service he took a job with a lumber company, and went off to the Virginia woods. Working for his board, he turned up the next autumn at the University of Michigan where he had the good fortune to come under the influence of Filibert Roth, author of the *First Book of Forestry,* a gifted German-born scholar and conservationist who influenced three generations of students. To be sure, the serious students of forestry then were not many; a classmate of McArdle's recalls that only nine took a degree in 1923. Summers they worked for the United States Forest Service at manual labor, sleeping in tents or shacks or on the ground, digging trenches to fight fires, following pack horses or pack mules into steep mountain country a hundred miles from railroads. To lean, six-foot McArdle those tough, muscular summers were sheer delight. They brought him back to Ann Arbor and Professor Roth each autumn with renewed hunger for direction.

During October of his senior year, he had need of it. Although his devotion to his profession was complete, he, like most college seniors, had begun to feel chill winds from the workaday world. He was a forester, but could he find a job? Could the nine members of his class find jobs? It was all very well to remember the excitement when Theodore Roosevelt and Gifford Pinchot led a crusade against plunderers of national resources, when Hamlin Garland made forest rangers the heroes of popular fiction. The 1920's were something else again. Under the Harding administration the cause of conservation had received many setbacks. Valuable public lands were leased corruptly to venal business interests; cabinet officers were bribed or betrayed their trust. Even respectable businessmen regarded conservation as the enemy of private enterprise, the impractical dream of cloistered idealists; when pressed, they could always fall back on the words of President Harding's successor, that laconic, eminently honest, no-nonsense son of Vermont, Calvin Coolidge:

"The business of America is business."

For the first time McArdle was worried. If there were any private timbering companies that hired foresters, he hadn't heard about them. He knew that some states had forestry departments but they were mainly small and ineffective, devoted principally to fire control. The only large employer was the Forest Service; it appeared to be fully staffed and, in view of public indifference to conservation, fighting at best a holding operation. Was there, McArdle wondered in his first wrestle with grave doubt, any real future for forestry in a country that seemed not to care? He took his problem to Professor Roth.

"Don't worry, McArdle," said Roth. "Wood is like bread, a necessity to the people. Because the country needs forests, it will always need foresters."

The United States Forest Service was the almost single-handed creation of an idealistic, driving, ambitious, impatient, egotistical, and sometimes capricious Pennsylvanian named Gifford Pinchot. As presently organized, it came into existence in 1905; the sponsoring legislation was enthusiastically supported by President Theodore Roosevelt, then at the peak of his power. But it was Pinchot, Roosevelt's friend and the first American to adopt forestry as a profession, who made the legislation possible. Next to Dwight L. Moody, he was possibly America's greatest and most effective evangelist.

It is interesting to discover from Pinchot's memoirs that just before he set off for Yale College in 1885 he was undecided between medicine and the ministry as a profession. It was his father, wealthy outdoors man, son of a Napoleonic soldier who emigrated to this country and prospered, who suggested he become a forester. But how become one? There were no forestry schools in this country and little interest in forests.

"Outside of the tropics," Pinchot wrote many years later, "American forests were the richest and most productive on earth, and the best able to repay good management. But nobody had begun to manage any part of them with an eye to the future. On the contrary, the greatest, the swiftest, the most efficient, and the most appalling wave of forest destruction in human history was then swelling to its climax in the United States; and the American people were glad of it. . . . More than 99 per cent of our people regarded forest perpetuation, if they thought about it at all, as needless and even ridiculous."

There were reasons for this attitude. The itching-footed New Englanders who moved on to Ohio and the Western Reserve, the Virginians who followed Boone and others through the water gaps to Tennessee and Kentucky, were primarily farmers. Timber had to be felled with ax and cross saw, stumps wedged out with infinite sweat and labor, to provide cleared tracts where the frontiersmen could grow crops to feed themselves and their livestock. The forest also meant to them fear and darkness and concealment for hostile Indians. What to do with timber? There was only one answer: Get rid of it.

Immediately after his graduation from Yale, Pinchot went abroad. In England friendly letters got him interviews with Sir William Schlich and Sir Dietrich Brandis, German-born English citizens who had been knighted for their services in establishing scientific forest management in British India. It was Brandis who became his guide and exemplar and advised him to study at the French forest school at Nancy. But when Pinchot came home, trained or (as he later admitted) half trained, he had a profession but no place to practice it.

"Forestry," Pinchot said then, and his definition still holds, "is tree farming. To grow trees as a crop is forestry. The farmer usually gets a crop every year from the land he farms. The forester may get his crop only once in thirty or fifty years but the harvested trees are the ones he planted. A well-handled farm gets more and more productive as the years pass. So does a well-handled forest."

Oddly enough, the crusading Pinchot got his first chance to prove the practicality of scientific management on the estate of an immensely rich man. George W. Vanderbilt was building himself a show place near Asheville, North Carolina; most of his enormous acreage was in woodland. He hired Pinchot as resident forester. The young enthusiast's accomplishments at Biltmore Forest were publicized both here and abroad. He not only restored a dying woodland but, by shrewd logging practices, made it pay.

Pinchot became chief of the tiny Forestry Division of the Department of Agriculture in 1898; he had ten people to work for him and no timber to manage. That was all changed a few years later when the national forest reserves were transferred from the Department of the Interior to his supervision. But the importance of Pinchot to this chapter is the imprint he left on the agency itself.

When "Tama Jim" Wilson, Secretary of Agriculture, invited him into government, he agreed that Pinchot could appoint his own assistants and that there would be neither political nor administrative interference. Wilson kept his word, and in Washington the tradition was soon established that the Forest Service was nonpolitical, fiercely independent, and untouchable. Most of the secretaries—Republicans and Democrats—who followed Wilson continued his hands-off policy.

Pinchot established another tradition when he surrounded himself with skilled and trained men and then gave them the freedom Wilson had given him. His assistant (and later his successor) was Henry S. Graves, a Yale graduate who was the second native American to become a professional forester. "We gave good men their heads," Pinchot wrote, "and the results were good." He early became convinced that direction from Washington could not solve immediate problems in the field. This was the origin of the Forest Service's present decentralized organization: the regional forester is in complete and unquestioned command of his region.

Pinchot was dismissed from the Forest Service by President Taft in 1910 as the result of Pinchot's thunderous and history-making hassle with Richard A. Ballinger, then Secretary of the Interior, over conservation policies. The issues and events involved are too complex for recital here, but the interested reader can find a mountain of material in any good public library. Pinchot was to continue active in public affairs, to serve twice as governor of Pennsylvania, and to live to great age.

When two members of his beloved agency called on him the year before his death, he put them off while he changed his clothes. He came stiffly down the stairs to meet them wearing his old green forester's uniform. His autobiography, *Breaking New Ground,* was published not long after. The year was 1947. This was the loyal, if not completely disinterested, dedication:

"To the men and women of the Forest Service, whose courage, devotion and intelligence have made it and kept it the best organization in the Government of the United States."

There are, of course, many other good organizations in the government, but the Forest Service has indeed been blessed with talented personnel. A roll call of the chiefs—Graves (who also created the Yale School of Forestry, which Pinchot family money financed), William B. Greeley, Robert Y. Stuart, F. A. Silcox, Earle H. Clapp, Lyle F. Watts, McArdle and his successor, Edward P. Cliff—is a roll call of talented men. Any one of them could have commanded in private industry three to five times the salary he earned in federal employment. So could most of their gifted assistants.

To refer to someone in government today as a "controversial figure" is to make trouble for him. The term has become, unhappily, a term of opprobrium. It means to many timid executives: "Better watch that guy!" Yet all the above-named men were, in one way or another, controversial figures. They stood for certain things, they stood up against other things, and often disagreed among themselves with asperity. It is interesting to note that all of them were professional foresters and came up through the ranks. The agency they guided enriched a nation while face-lifting its geography.

Richard McArdle became Chief of the Forest Service in July, 1952. But his introduction to the doctrine of independent responsibility came long before that. Fresh out of college, he had just reported for duty in Portland, Oregon. A forest fire was raging in the foothills and he was instructed to recruit fire fighters from Portland's Skid Row. He got his fire fighters—such as they were—embarked them on hired buses, and then telephoned his office for further instructions. His boss was crisp. "McArdle," he said, "It's your fire now."

The resourceful young man who met the crisis at 88, rue de l'Université met this crisis, but he still remembers the cold perspiration of fear and inexperience. In these more enlightened days a neophyte would never be called upon to direct fire fighting—the risks are too immediate—but McArdle is not sure his hazing was wrong. Because he had to make decisions, he made them. And he has been making them ever since.

McArdle was born in Lexington, Kentucky, but moved at an early age to Norfolk. His father, a native of Rushville, Indiana, was a custom tailor who made an adequate living for his family and was active in Boy Scout work. McArdle was active also, and, as befits an Eagle Scout, continues to be extremely deft with his hands. Give him scissors and folded pieces of paper, and he will produce for his grandchildren or the children of friends a variety of dazzling figures to adorn their scrapbooks.

Today he looks back with no regrets on a lifetime romance with public service. During his adult years he never worked for a private employer, yet he has almost as many friends and admirers in industry as in government. So far as personal satisfaction is concerned, he reached a high point when he organized the Fifth World Forestry Congress, which was held at Seattle in 1960. Sixty-five nations sent delegations, and there were 2,000 participants. McArdle was elected president of the Congress. Here also are some of the official awards that have come his way:

Distinguished Service, Department of Agriculture, 1957; Career Service award, National Civil Service League, 1958; Distinguished Service, American Forestry Association, 1958; Distinguished Service, Forest Farmers' Association,

1959; Award for Merit, Public Personnel Association, 1959; Distinguished Service, New York State College of Forestry, 1961; Rockefeller Public Service Award, 1961; Distinguished Federal Civilian Service, President's Gold Medal, 1961; Order of Merit for Forestry of Miguel Angel de Quevado, Government of Mexico, 1961; Sir William Schlich Memorial Medal, 1962; Order of Merit, Federal Republic of Germany, 1962.

When McArdle received his German Order of Merit he did not forget his indebtedness to Filibert Roth. He spoke of "Daddy" Roth's influence on all his students, and his inculcation of high ideals in the aspiring young.

"This is not something," McArdle said, "that can be scheduled as a special course; it should be in every course. It's not something to be taught out of a book. Idealism is something which has to be caught, like measles, and a student won't catch it unless his teacher has it."

On one occasion McArdle, rarely sentimental, spoke of his pilgrimage to the former Duchy of Württemberg, where Roth had grown up. "I thought I felt a hand on my shoulder," he said, "as I walked through his native woods."

Richard McArdle received his federal appointment as a junior forester in 1924. He had completed undergraduate studies in three years, and won a master's degree in science the following year. He was an excellent student, popular on the campus, but—a war veteran and a little older than his classmates—he was amiably indifferent to such juvenilia as campus politics and social fraternities. He was not even much impressed later with his title as assistant silviculturist at the Northwest Forest Experiment Station at

Portland. He already knew he had a lot to learn, that his ultimate aim was not to fight forest fires but to do research. He was to do both. In 1927 he went back to Michigan as a part-time instructor, and in 1930 received his Ph.D. degree. In 1934-35 he was granted a leave of absence from government and served for a year as Dean of the School of Forestry at the University of Idaho.

When McArdle returned to the Forest Service he became Director of the Rocky Mountain Forest and Range Experiment Station at Fort Collins, Colorado, and, subsequently, of the Appalachian Forest Experiment Station at Asheville, North Carolina. In 1944 he was called to Washington and became Assistant Chief of the Forest Service in charge of state and private forestry cooperation. Eight years later he succeeded Lyle F. Watts as Chief.

Few people in the ordinary walks of life have any real conception of the sweep and scope of this post. The Chief is responsible for the administration and protection of 154 national forests and national grasslands in forty-one states and Puerto Rico. These federal properties add up to 186 million acres—about one tenth of the whole area of the United States. They are revenue-producing: timber sales, grazing fees, and other services bring in more than $100 million a year. And as national wealth, tangible and intangible, their value is incalculable.

More than half the water supply of the western states (for example) originates on these public lands; western agriculture and industry are dependent on the flow from mountain watersheds. One third of the country's big game and wildlife inhabit the national forests; there are 81,000 miles of fishing streams and nearly three million acres of natural lakes and impounded waters. Millions of cattle and sheep graze government-owned range. Because of America's increased leisure, recreational use multiplies each year. Hunters, fishermen, hikers, tourists of every description now make more than 100 million visits annually.

The Forest Service plants approximately two billion trees a year, and provides technical assistance to private landowners who request it. In addition to policing its own preserves, the Service cooperates in the control of fire on 400 million acres of state and independently owned forest lands. For decades it has provided leadership in planning and directing forestry research, and, indeed, pioneered in the new methods of forest utilization that have revolutionized the timber industry. Research is centered at ten regional experiment stations and at the Forest Products Laboratory at Madison, Wisconsin.

Of all this, Richard McArdle was part and parcel for thirty-nine years, first as a summer roustabout, then as a research scientist, finally as administrator, policy maker, and boss of the whole shebang. The Forest Service he entered was a small, compact agency temporarily isolated from the rough-and-tumble of contention and politics by the very geographic isolation and loneliness of its field work. In the 1920's there were approximately 2,500 permanent employees. Now there are more than 18,000—with seasonal employment of 14,000 more in summer.

Congresses and Presidents brought vast new acreages under public control during the intervening years, and changing times brought new responsibilities once unimaginable. What ranger of Teddy Roosevelt's era could have dreamed that tens of thousands of tourists would one day poke motorcars and trailers into timber solitudes that seemed equidistant from Washington and the moon? Or that there would be ski slopes where once the Nez Percés hunted?

One thing, of course, never changes: the thorny relationship between government and the cattle and sheep men. Government regulation of government lands rarely suits ranchers, all of them individualists, who want to lease more and more grazing acres and put more and more livestock on those acres. They have spokesmen in Congress who regularly introduce bills that would permit unrestricted grazing. A few years ago I spent a winter in the Southwest and asked a Tucson banker for an independent opinion. Did he, a Westerner, think the government acted tyrannically or unreasonably in its dealings with private stockmen?

"If the grazing policy were relaxed," he said, "northern Arizona would be desert within three years—but please don't quote me."

The principle of "multiple use of the forest" has been gospel to the Forest Service since its beginnings, but, increasingly, it makes life miserable for administrators. Stockmen want more grazing; loggers want more trees to cut at lower government prices; recreation associations want more skiing, swimming, and camping areas; and wilderness enthusiasts (equally hoggish in their own idealistic way) seem to want the forests put under lock and key with admission tickets available—as a friend of mine phrased it

—only to Supreme Court Justice William O. Douglas and Chippewa Indians in birchbark canoes.

A few years after he became Chief, McArdle found himself in the middle of a long-time controversy over the Three Sisters Wilderness Area in Oregon. The Three Sisters are mountain peaks along the backbone of the Cascades in Oregon, and the 191,000 acres originally proscribed are in rough, primitive country. Subsequently some 50,000 acres were added to the wilderness area. This addition, McArdle told me, was commonplace country, without scenic value, and should have been managed for multiple use in the first place. In a primitive area, according to regulation, roads cannot be built and commercial timber cutting is prohibited.

McArdle wanted those 50,000 commonplace acres restored to multiple use so he could provide access to the wilderness area in case of fire, and provide more accessibility to hikers and climbers. He ruled against many of his friends in Congress and in the wilderness organizations; some of them haven't forgiven him since.

Conservation programs take patience; it is often years before they come to fruition. When McArdle became director at Fort Collins, Colorado, in 1935, he instituted a sweeping research program that has only just reached its culmination. The western slope of the Rockies is a "humic island" which, through the Rio Grande and the Colorado and other streams, feeds water to the parched Great Plains. The job McArdle set for himself was to devise means to increase that water flow.

This included study of coniferous forests in the high snows, experimental methods of cutting, thorough investigation of snow-melt over many seasons. The results of this research have been spectacular: water flow has been increased 25 per cent.

How was it done? Trees were cut in alternate strips in the high forest, leaving cleared spaces between the lines of uncut trees. Because of the open spaces thus created, snow that would have stayed semipermanently in the tree-tops, or been lost by evaporation in the upper atmosphere, fell to the ground and melted. Any added water supply helps to assure the success of such exciting projects as the Reclamation Service's "Big Thompson" diversion. Water from the western slopes of the Rockies is carried in tunnels through the mountains to the arid eastern slope and made available for irrigation farming in the Denver and western Nebraska area.

Development of fire-fighting techniques has been of paramount interest to the Forest Service throughout its history. The disastrous conflagrations that swept the states of Oregon, Washington, Montana, Idaho, and eastern Minnesota in 1910 enlisted national support and produced appropriations from Congress. Some three million acres were burned over, and eighty-five fire fighters and civilians were killed. One of the heroes was a ranger named Edward C. Pulaski, whose knowledge of the hills saved forty-two entrapped fire fighters from death; he led them to an abandoned mine tunnel. He later invented a fire-fighting tool known to this day as the "pulaski." It combines the features of an ax and a grub hoe and is a primary tool in every fire fighter's kit.

Control methods were vastly improved during the 1930's. The late Harry T. Gisborne deserves the credit for much of this work, but McArdle did his part. One of the ways of putting out a blaze in a hurry is to spot it while still small. But smoke plays queer tricks with the optical transparency of the atmosphere; unless the lookout man in the tower on the peak knows the amount of haze in the air, he may be dangerously deceived about geography and distance—as much as the difference between ten miles and two miles. McArdle's contribution, developed in collaboration with young physicists from Reed College, was a haze meter that assisted accurate observation.

Forecasting of fire hazard was another development. This is made possible by the collection and correlation of weather factors. Is the vegetation green or dry? What are the rainfall figures? Temperature and humidity? Wind direction? Condition of the pine needles and other timber litter? In the forest-fire season every regional forester receives day-to-day statistics from his outposts by telephone and short-wave radio, computes the "danger rating" in each locality. These intelligences tell him where trouble is most likely to occur and permit him to assemble and deploy his fire-fighting forces before the emergency is actually at hand.

One of the field man's adjuncts is a device known as the moisture indicator stick, another advance to which McArdle contributed. Two types of wood are used for moisture sticks—basswood in the eastern United States, ponderosa pine in the West—because they most accurately report local conditions. These sticks, which have been artificially aged to remove resins, are placed on wire bases some ten inches above the ground. Twice a day they are weighed on special scales. This gives the ranger a reasonably accurate picture of the moisture content—and the combustibility—of the forest litter in the vicinity.

Perhaps the most dramatic modern innovation is fire fighting from the air. On July 12, 1940, near Martin Creek in Montana, two men made the first parachute drop to combat a timber fire. Since that time there have been more than 27,000 jumps without a fatality. One of the men who dreamed up the program was a personal friend of the writer, the late David P. Godwin. And so successful was the program that, at the beginning of World War II, Major William Carey Lee adopted Forest Service ideas and procedures and organized the Army's first parachute training at Fort Benning, Georgia.

Smoke jumpers are recruited early each spring. A majority of the candidates are college students. Mental and physical standards are high: recruits must have had at least one season of fire-fighting experience, must be self-reliant and accustomed to a rugged outdoor life. Successful candidates are given a four-weeks course and then assigned to smoke-jumper bases. Each base has special maneuverable planes and helicopters that enable the jumpers to reach fires quickly—sometimes only a few minutes after the fires are reported.

During McArdle's administration as Chief, another major breakthrough was made in fire control. In 1956 the Forest Service and cooperating state agencies dropped or cascaded water and chemicals from airplanes on twenty-three California fires. A squadron of small craft equipped with 100-gallon tanks and special discharge gates dropped 123,000 gallons of water and fire-retardant sodium calcium

borate (bentonite is an even newer retardant); this air support was the deciding factor in suppressing fourteen of the
twenty-three fires.

Since then the program has been improved and broadened. Helicopters are used to lay hose connected to ground
trucks. In one experiment it took a ground crew of eight
men thirty minutes to lay 1,500 feet of hose up a 70 percent slope. A helicopter did the job in fifty-three seconds.
The carrying capacities of the tankers of the air have been
greatly increased, and in one recent year they cascaded
more than two million gallons of "slurry"—water mixed
with chemicals—on smoking woodlands beneath.

Statistics offer convincing proof of the progress made in
thirty years. In 1932 there were 140,722 authenticated forest fires on public and private lands, and (an appalling
total) almost 44 million acres burned. In 1962 there were
115,345 fires in a dry and dangerous season, and four million acres burned. Since 1958, fires annually have averaged
about 100,000 in number, and annual devastation hovers
around the four-million-acre mark.

In the mid-1950's, research and control activities on forest insect diseases—a protection perhaps as important as
protection from fire—were transferred to McArdle's agency
from other sections of the Agriculture Department. DDT
is still extensively used, but the demonstrated side effects
of DDT (a bow here to Miss Rachel Carson, author of
Silent Spring) have led to profitable investigations into
nonchemical fields. For instance, a predator wasp has been
imported from Europe that feeds on a pest known as the
balsam woolly aphid. And a virus spray spread by airplane

has been effective against a defoliating insect called the pine sawfly.

In June, 1960, the Forest Products Laboratory at Madison celebrated its golden anniversary. It was the first, and for several years the only, institution conducting research on wood as a commercial product; other nations have since followed American leadership and developed laboratories along similar lines. In a half century the Madison experts have pioneered in the development of laminated wood, plywood, glues, paints, wood cellulose, and the utilization of so-called trash trees and hardwoods for pulp-paper requirements.

Commercial builders everywhere are in profound debt to the laboratory. The prefabricated-house industry owes its period of gold-plated prosperity to the stressed-skin construction principle that was developed at Madison; more than 150,000 houses a year are now built according to these design truisms. An even later discovery is sandwich-panel construction that combines light weight with strength and rigidity. Originally it was useful to the aircraft industry; lately it has been useful in the field of guided missiles, housing construction, and the building of trucks, trailers, and railroad cars.

Another of McArdle's achievements was his leadership of the fight to revise outmoded mining laws; they had not been effectively changed since 1892. Astonishingly enough, the claimant of a mining claim in the national forests had exclusive rights not only to subsurface minerals but to the surface itself. He could prevent the government from building roads across his claim and harvesting timber there. About 1,200,000 mining claims had been located on national forest lands. Each claim covered twenty acres; that meant that about 24 million acres in national forest areas were not controlled by the Forest Service.

Actually, many of the claimants had no interest in minerals; they were interested in harvesting the commercial timber growing there. Or they were interested in the land itself as residential or industrial property—or in the black-mail value of blocking a right-of-way for access roads. In the San Bernardino Forest in California, for example, many mining claims were used as locations for summer homes; in other places they were used as sites for stores and motels, without even a scratch in a hill to indicate search for minerals.

The American Mining Congress in the past had opposed changes in the mining laws. After McArdle presented his program at a joint meeting of representatives of the Mining Congress and the American Forestry Association—and presented it forcefully—the Congress elected to support his reforms. The Multiple Use Mining Law was passed July 23, 1955. The measure, among other things, authorized a review of existing claims on public lands by cooperating federal agencies. This has been a long and arduous task, which the Forest Service predicted would take ten years for completion. By June, 1963, it was 96 per cent completed, and 50 billion feet of timber had been returned to Forest Service control. Only a small percentage of the so-called claim holders made any effort to defend their illusory "rights." It was estimated that, when the job was finished, the Forest Service would manage surface resources on all but about 4,000 of the 1,200,000 claims.

*

"The Forest Service didn't join me," McArdle said recently. "I joined the Forest Service. Long before I came along, it had well-developed standards of competence, thoroughness, devotion to public service. If I wanted to stay, I had to meet those standards."

During his ten years as Chief he served under three Secretaries of Agriculture: Charles F. Brannan of Colorado, Ezra Taft Benson of Utah, and Orville L. Freeman of Minnesota. Three more different men in political philosophy, personality, and (perhaps) even sensory reaction to hot and cold would be hard to find. Yet McArdle managed to get along with them all, to protect his agency from political sharpshooting, to guide prudently the expansion that new tasks and new responsibilities made necessary.

When Benson, an avowed conservative, came into office with the Republicans, many career men in the technical branches of the Department of Agriculture were dubious and resentful. Some of Benson's personal associates had said arrogantly and publicly that "we will now get a full day's work for a full day's pay." McArdle, who had been in the top post for only six months, sought and obtained a personal interview with the Secretary.

McArdle spoke plainly but without heat. He pointed out that the continuity of service and scientific knowledge of career people were vital to a new Cabinet officer; he needed their loyalty and competence. So far as he, McArdle, was concerned, the time might come when his services could be dispensed with, but he did not believe an immediate resignation would serve either Benson or the efficiency of the Forest Service.

"If you give me the chance," he said, "I will continue

to make my recommendations. There will be no end runs. The final decisions will be yours, and I will abide by those decisions as long as, in conscience and responsibility, I can. When I can't, I'll get out."

McArdle recalls that Benson looked at him silently for a moment and then shook his hand. They never discussed the matter again.

Like his predecessors, McArdle was raised on the Pinchot doctrine that forest resources could be protected only by federal regulation—that is, federal regulation of timber-cutting on both public and *private* lands. Many experts in the field came to believe that this was outworn gospel or, at best, unachievable. The large lumber companies had already learned conservation; they regularly practiced reforestation, and the work was supervised by university-trained foresters on their own payrolls. But hostility between government and industry continued to exist.

During the war and postwar years McArdle did much to ease this hostility and to improve cooperation with state forestry departments. Of his appointment to the top job, Henry C. Clepper has written in the *Journal of Forestry:* "He could not have taken office at a more fortuitous time. A forester of his professional stature, equable disposition, and compromising ability was needed."

Without formally repudiating the doctrine of regulation—which, incidentally, no Congress had ever seriously considered—McArdle sought to gain his ends by example and persuasion, and with success. He proved himself shrewd, informed, diplomatic, and determined. Other qualities won him unswerving loyalty from subordinates: kindness, genuine concern for their welfare, a willingness to take advice and counsel. Every year he faithfully followed what he called "the potato salad circuit," which meant he visited and picnicked with employees and their families in all the Forest Service's far-flung, and often completely isolated, outposts.

Back in 1956 President Eisenhower went out to Montana to dedicate the new parachute-training installation at Missoula. During his speech he remarked that he had recently visited a Forest Service station where a talented cook named Andy O'Malia had baked him a much-appreciated Boston cream pie. Then the President turned to McArdle, who was also on the platform.

"Within the last week," he said, "I have had a little proof of the qualities of leadership of Mr. McArdle. It has not been my good fortune to know him. But only two nights ago, in Fraser, Colorado, I was visited at my cabin by the cook. And he said: 'I read in the paper you are going to Missoula. There you will see my boss, Mr. McArdle. Give him my greetings and best wishes.'

"I was long with the Army, and I have seen some of the finest battle units that have ever been produced; and whenever you find one where the cook and the private in the ranks want to be remembered to the General, then you know it is a good outfit. I pay my salute to Mr. McArdle."

McArdle retired on St. Patrick's Day, 1962, after he had made sure that Secretary Freeman would appoint a career forester to succeed him. When he left the Service, at sixty-three, his dark hair was only threaded with gray; he lived with his wife (whom he met when both were students at the University of Michigan) in a big old-fashioned house in northwest Washington that periodically bulged with grandchildren. Two of his sons were educated as foresters. One served as a Forest Service ranger in the wilds of Idaho; the other switched allegiance after military service and worked for the Defense Department. A third son is a geographer by profession.

Out of government, McArdle continued to be closely tied to government affairs. He spent much time as executive secretary of the National Institute of Public Affairs, a nonprofit organization financed by the Ford Foundation that sponsors a program of career education awards for government employees.

When Dr. McArdle was told in 1963 that he was one of eight Rockefeller Public Service Award winners who were to sit for their literary portraits, he sent a worried letter to Dr. R. W. van de Velde, Faculty Secretary of the Woodrow Wilson School of Public Administration, at Princeton, which administers these awards. McArdle didn't like the idea.

"I cannot help but wish," he wrote, "that the project was not being done." He was more interested than most in recruiting talented young people for government employment, he said, but he was not convinced that the publicizing of a few would do the job.

"I'm afraid you would stress my influence on the Forest Service and what I did as an individual. I hope that I did my share in shaping this one unit of government. Of more significance is what the Forest Service did to shape me.

"Despite what some people think, a public agency such as the Forest Service is not an amorphous mass. It has shape, character, individuality. This is not the work of one person but of many over a long period, and these qualities are not radically changed by any one person. In turn, the character of the agency (if it's any good) shapes the character of those who work there.

"My philosophy of public service was not originated by me—I had no such philosophy at the start—but was created and nurtured by the Forest Service in accordance with a sort of group philosophy developed over a long time by many people. You won't find this in any official or unofficial manual, regulation, or handbook. So far as I remember, no one even talked to me about the agency's attitude toward public service. But let no one try to tell you that I wasn't 'molded'; there were times when I could feel the mold pressing in on me.

"So it is, too, with other characteristics of an agency—its standards of personal and agency integrity, of accuracy and thoroughness, and many other qualities which we ordinarily think of as purely personal.

"As Chief I was a lot more sensitive and responsive to 'public opinion' inside the Service than I was to public opinion outside it. I had hundreds of deeply interested (and knowledgeable) inspectors—the whole rank and file of the Forest Service—looking at everything I did, checking, for example, if a decision was in the best interest of the greatest number of people over the long pull, or for the temporary benefit of a favored few.

"If I were a young man, I would deliberately try to pick a government agency with high standards—for the same reason a tennis player likes to compete against more skillful players. It's fun to improve your game."

Notes About the Authors

HOWARD SIMONS (Hugh L. Dryden) is a science writer who has reported many of the major events of the space age for the *Washington Post* and its associated newspapers. In 1961 he won the $1,000 award, sponsored jointly by the Westinghouse Electric Corporation and the American Association for the Advancement of Science, for the best science writing of the year. While he was news editor of Science Service in 1958, he won a Nieman Fellowship to Harvard University. His articles, mostly on scientific subjects, have appeared in *Harper's*, the *Saturday Evening Post*, the *Saturday Review*, and other magazines. He was born in Albany, New York, and is a graduate of Union College and the Columbia School of Journalism.

WALLACE CARROLL (Llewellyn E. Thompson), foreign correspondent and newspaper editor, reported from Europe for the United Press before and during World War II. Later in the war, he directed the United States government's information program in Britain and then its psychological warfare operations in Europe. He re-entered to daily journalism in 1949 as executive news editor of the *Journal* and *Sentinel* in Winston-Salem, North Carolina; in 1955 he became Washington news editor of *The New York Times;* and in 1963 returned to Winston-Salem to be editor and publisher of the two newspapers there. As a foreign correspondent, he had watched Llewellyn Thompson's career in prewar Geneva, and later in Moscow when the Nazi army was hammering at the gates of the Soviet capital. He has served as a consultant to government departments and as a lecturer at the National War College and other service academies. The books he has written are *We're in This with Russia,* published in wartime, and *Persuade or Perish,* a study of psychological warfare.

GOVE HAMBIDGE (Sterling Hendricks), writer and editor, was most recently a founder of the Society for International Development and editor of its *International Development Review.* Earlier, he worked with the United Nations Food and Agriculture Organization from 1945 to 1955, first as director of information, then as North American regional representative. Before 1945 he spent ten years with the United States Department of Agriculture, editing the first seven of the new *Yearbooks of Agriculture* started by Henry A. Wallace—each a 1,000-page symposium on a major field of agricultural science. He also served as the Co-ordinator of Research Information in the department. For ten years previously he had been a free-lance writer for major magazines and radio stations. He is the author of seven books, four of them personal, three reportorial.

E. W. KENWORTHY (Colin F. Stam) has, since 1957, been reporting on the Congress, the White House, and the

State Department for *The New York Times.* He began his career as a teacher of English, first at Oberlin College and Western Reserve Academy; after receiving an M.A. in English literature at Brown University, he continued teaching at Classical High School in Providence, Rhode Island, and at Indiana University Extension. His work in goverment began in 1943 as a writer in the Office of War Information; it continued as First Secretary of the U.S. Embassy in London (1946-47) and as Executive Secretary of President Truman's Committee on Equality of Treatment and Opportunity in the Armed Services (1949-50). In addition to reporting for *The New York Times,* his journalistic work has included writing editorials for the *Baltimore Evening Sun* (1945-56) and a stint with the *Reporter* (1948-49). He joined the staff of *The New York Times* "News of the Week in Review" in 1950, and moved to the Washington bureau seven years later.

GEORGE R. STEWART (Thomas B. Nolan), author of *Fire, Storm,* and many other works of fiction and nonfiction, has had an almost lifelong interest in the West and its natural treasures. For his writings on California he received the silver medal of the Commonwealth Club of that state in 1936 and the gold medal two years later. He was chairman of the advisory committee for the California Place-Names Project in 1944-47, and a collaborator of the United States Forest Service in 1945-46. Recently he retired, as Professor Emeritus, from the Department of English at the University of California (Berkeley) after almost forty years on its teaching staff. In 1963, that university awarded him the degree of Doctor of Humane Letters. Honors from other universities have come his way, among them an appointment to Princeton in 1942 as Resident Fellow in creative writing, and, a decade later, another as Fulbright Professor of American Literature at the University of Athens.

HERBERT C. YAHRAES, Jr. (Robert H. Felix) has written articles for many national magazines and pamphlets for the Public Affairs Committee and the National Institutes of Health. Several of his articles have been included in collections of readings for sociology students; others have brought citations for science writing. With his wife, Dixie, who often works with him, he received a Lasker award for medical writings in magazines. He has been an editorial consultant to the Operations Research Office of Johns Hopkins University and to the National Capital Transportation Agency. Earlier, as a newspaperman, he covered Huey Long in Louisiana for the New Orleans *Item* and *Tribune,* served eight years with the Associated Press in New York, and edited the Sunday Magazine of Ralph Ingersoll's *PM.* In 1943-44 he was a Nieman Fellow at Harvard.

OSCAR SCHISGALL (Robert M. Ball), in a long and successful writing career, has contributed almost 3,000 articles to all the major American magazines. Apart from his magazine writing, Mr. Schisgall is the author of twenty-nine books and of a number of motion picture and television dramas. During World War II he served as chief of the book and magazine bureau of the Office of War Information. Later, returning to the ranks of free-lance writers, he won a Benjamin Franklin award for public service with his magazine articles. Mr. Schisgall and his wife, Lillian, who collaborates with him in most of his work, reside in New York City. The literary tradition they established has been continued by their sons, a physician and a lawyer, both of whom have published a number of articles.

MILTON MacKAYE (Richard E. McArdle) is a former newspaperman and an experienced free-lance reporter who has been contributing articles on governmental and political affairs to the national magazines for many years. He was one of the originators of the famous "Profiles" in *The New Yorker;* his articles have also appeared in the *Saturday Evening Post, Scribner's, McCall's, Ladies' Home Journal, Redbook, Reader's Digest,* and *Holiday.* Among his several books, *Our Jungle Road to Tokyo,* written in collaboration with the late General R. L. Eichelberger, received high critical acclaim. His wife is Dorothy Cameron Disney, a novelist and journalist in her own right, and they live in Washington, D.C., and Madison, Connecticut. During World War II, MacKaye was a writer for the Office of War Information, a special assistant to the Under Secretary of War, the late Robert P. Patterson, and director of publications for the Office of War Information in London.

DELIA AND FERDINAND KUHN (the editors) have served in the United States government and have also reported many of its activities at home and abroad. For ten years during and after World War II, Mrs. Kuhn was a civil servant in the State Department, the Office of War Information, and the Technical Co-operation Administration ("Point Four"). Her husband interrupted his newspaper career in 1941 to be an assistant to the Secretary of the Treasury and later a deputy director of the Office of War Information. Both have had long experience in journalism. Before her marriage, Mrs. Kuhn was associate editor of *Current History* magazine and was an assistant to the managing editor of *The New Yorker.* Mr. Kuhn was London correspondent of *The New York Times* before the war, and from 1946 to 1953 covered foreign affairs as diplomatic correspondent of the *Washington Post.* Since 1953 the Kuhns have collaborated as free-lance writers, reporting from distant lands and contributing to

Collier's, Harper's, Holiday, the *National Geographic,* and other magazines. They are joint authors of *Borderlands* (1962), a book about some of the regions of Asia where their work has taken them.

A Postscript for Young Readers
WHO MAY BE PONDERING
GOVERNMENT CAREERS

The stories you have read of eight outstanding federal career men tell in themselves what makes government service so worth while. Despite frustration, stretches of dullness, and sometimes seemingly insurmountable barriers, there is, among government servants, a sense of fulfillment encountered in few other jobs—"a warming sense of the importance of their work in the scheme of things."

How does one go about entering the federal service? What are the requirements, opportunities, rewards? This section offers some practical answers.

Never has the federal government been more interested in recruiting talented young people, and never has government work been more stimulating than it is now. For men and women of ability and training, working in the public service has some enormous advantages: interesting jobs, opportunities for steady advancement, security, stimulating colleagues, better pay than most people realize, and again—most important —the real satisfaction that comes from knowing you are serving your country.

Not everyone can qualify for public service, but those who do stand an excellent chance of finding the kind of work and rewards they seek. Over 90 per cent of federal jobs are under the Civil Service personnel system, and, in addition, the Foreign Service has a merit system of its own. That means jobs and promotions are based on performance, not political "pull" or social standing. People who are appointed on the basis of their ability to do the work continue to do it, so long as they remain capable, under succeeding national administrations, without fear of job loss for political reasons.

Qualified applicants also are considered without regard to race, creed, national origin, or sex. You qualify by demonstrating your ability in competitive examinations. And, interestingly enough, no matter what you study—from agronomy to political science, accounting to geology, from astrophysics to economics—there probably is a job for you in federal government if you are good enough to compete successfully and get a high grade in the qualifying exam. The variety of work under Civil Service is enormous—hundreds of different kinds of jobs in some seventy departments and agencies. Yet few students apparently realize, when they specialize in something other than public administration, that they may really be preparing for government careers.

ENTRANCE EXAMINATIONS

Three general kinds of competitive examinations open the door to jobs in government at the beginning professional level.
   1. The Federal Service Entrance Examination.
   2. Professional entrance-level examinations for specialists.
   3. Annual Foreign Service written examinations.

THE FEDERAL SERVICE EXAM

This examination is held several times each year to fill positions in some sixty occupational fields for jobs throughout the country and overseas. Note: The majority of government career jobs are NOT in Washington, D.C. Almost $2\frac{1}{4}$ million people work outside Washington, and only 258,000 in the District of Columbia itself. Thus 90 per cent are scattered around the country and the world.

The FSEE is open to all college graduates and to juniors and seniors in college, regardless of their major fields of study. It is also open to what may be termed "college caliber" people who for some reason have not gone to college. The purpose of the exam is to find those young people who have the potential to grow and develop and become career managers, skilled technicians, and professional leaders tomorrow. More than 10,000 positions are filled each year from the FSEE.

Those who pass this test become trainees in their first positions. The written exam, which takes about $3\frac{1}{2}$ hours, is a test of general abilities. The training program that follows defines your specialized aptitudes and interests. You may be a trainee in administration, economics, biology, statistics, social science, press relations, business analysis, agriculture, personnel management—you name it.

The federal agencies regard trainee jobs as steppingstones for career employees who demonstrate that they are ready for more responsible work. In this they resemble the apprenticeships of our grandfathers' times, except that trainees advance more rapidly. Government workers receive automatic increases every fifty-two weeks in the early part of their careers and every seventy-eight weeks when they attain higher grades, if their work is at an acceptable level of competence.

You can even be a trainee on a temporary basis (130 days a year during the summer) if you want to try your wings in federal service while still an undergraduate. You must be pursuing courses related to the field in which you seek a summer appointment. Write directly to the agency that interests you.

Management Internships: The FSEE also is used to recruit promising people with management potential for special training as "management interns." Candidates for these must first take the FSEE and then an *additional,* more difficult written test. Having passed this successfully, they must qualify further in a group interview. This consists of gathering seven or eight applicants around a table to discuss a problem suggested by the examiner, who then observes their reactions and rates them accordingly. Personal recommendations from former teachers or employers also play a part in qualifying candidates for internships.

Obviously, not a large number of interns are selected each year. But those who make the grade are given special training of from a few to eighteen months after their appointments. This training consists of planned work assignments, special projects, and counsel regarding further study outside of working hours.

Salaries: Trainee jobs in 1963 started at between $4,500 and $5,500 a year, with outstanding candidates getting the higher amount. Management interns began at from $5,500 to almost $6,700, the higher rate paid usually to those who had completed a year of graduate work or had comparable experience. Civil Service over-all pay rates run from about $3,200 in the lowest grade to $20,000 in the highest.

PROFESSIONAL ENTRANCE-LEVEL EXAMINATIONS

Some jobs are filled through special examinations announced under specific job titles for people who are trained as engineers, chemists, physicists, librarians, accountants, auditors, etc. These exams may be announced by the central or regional offices of the Civil Service Commission. You can find out about them also at your college placement office or by writing directly to your nearest U.S. Civil Service Commission office. (Look it up under "U.S. Government" in the telephone book.)

A number of federal jobs are *excepted* from Civil Service requirements, including some in agencies that operate their *own* merit systems, such as the Tennessee Valley Authority, the Atomic Energy Commission, the Federal Bureau of Investigation. Applications for such positions should be made directly to the agencies.

FOREIGN SERVICE EXAMINATIONS

The Department of State recruits men and women for Foreign Service careers through its own written and oral competitive examinations given each September. Candidates must be between twenty-one and thirty-one years old, have been American citizens for at least nine years and, if married, be married to an American citizen.

Foreign Service officers, those on-the-spot observers who deal with other governments and report on conditions in other countries that affect the interests of the U.S., specialize in such fields as economics, public and business administration, languages, geography, history, and political science. Application forms must be sent in during July. You can get the forms from the Board of Examiners of the Department of State, Washington 25, D.C.

Foreign Service has always been considered the "glamour girl" of the federal agencies insofar as jobs are concerned. It is demanding but fascinating work. Young people who think of it in terms of the more sophisticated capitals of the world, such as Paris, London, Rome, Buenos Aires, should realize that members of the Foreign Service work in 300 embassies, legations, and consulates in more than 100 countries. The distant posts are often the most interesting. Opportunities for a young Foreign Service officer really to do a job are greater in new countries, even if living conditions vary widely. Africa and Southeast Asia are considered by those who serve there as the most challenging posts of all.

If you are qualified for the job of protecting American citizens and interests abroad, you do not have to have people in high places recommend you, as is commonly believed. Virtually all professional positions in the diplomatic and consular posts abroad are filled by Foreign Service officers who have qualified for appointment through the examinations.

Your work in the Foreign Service would acquaint you with every aspect of the life of the countries to which you were assigned. You would meet people from all levels of action and opinion, gain your experience through political and economic analysis of local and international events; by reporting on commerce, trade, labor, education, and culture; by searching for new markets for U.S. products and by bargaining down foreign tariffs and trade restrictions against them; by working to help individual Americans abroad in difficulties of a thousand kinds; and generally by working day and night to win friends and understanding of your country's policies abroad. *Salaries:* Junior Foreign Service officers earn from about $6,200 to $8,200 a year, with supplementary allowances for quarters abroad unless they live in government-owned quarters. They also receive a cost-of-living allowance when stationed at posts where it costs more to live than in Washington, D.C. Ambassadors can earn up to $27,500 plus provision of housing and an entertainment allowance. Career ministers can earn $19,800, and first secretaries from $14,260 to $19,650.

OTHER OPPORTUNITIES

It is obviously impossible in an appendix this brief to list all the kinds of jobs available to young men and women in the federal government, much less the comparable positions that are open in state and municipal governments, which also operate (in some places) by the competitive merit system. If you are interested in a more detailed description, write for "Federal Careers, a Directory for College Students," Superintendent of Documents, Washington 25, D.C. (cost: 60 cents). It contains word-and-picture stories of the work of the federal agencies and the career opportunities in each.

Here are some of the opportunities in fields of public service to which the eight subjects of this book have contributed directly or indirectly:

Physical Science and Engineering: A wide variety of engineering and scientific programs exists in the federal government, challenging the skill, imagination, and knowledge of professionally prepared people. In 1963 the government needed 5,000 new engineers, 2,500 graduates in physics, chemistry, mathematics, and other physical science specialties. True, private industry also is seeking these people, but it must be remembered that some of the outstanding developments of our time have come about through brilliant and dedicated government careerists of the sort who have won Rockefeller Public Service Awards.

Among the developments to which government scientists have made major contributions are heat-resistant ceramic coatings for space vehicles and aircraft; supersonic plane design; missile and aircraft warning systems; earth satellites; disease-preventing drugs and vaccines; electronic computers.

Men and women who have received their degrees in the science field need take no written tests for jobs with starting salaries of over $5,500 for holders of bachelor's degrees or $6,600 if the scholastic record is superior. Candidates with two years of graduate study may start at over $7,100.

Accounting: The size and diversity of government activities are measured in billions of dollars. That is one reason why government careers appeal to a large number of well-trained accountants with imagination and skill. They operate extensive audit programs, design cost-accounting systems for public utilities, financial institutions, insurance activities, and warehouses.

A person with a liking for numbers and the kinds of occupations mentioned above must obtain training as an accountant before applying for a government career job in this field. This means four years of college study with at least twenty-four semester hours in accounting, but no written test is required and ratings are based on training and experience.

Salaries: Entrance salaries range from around $5,000 for trainees to $14,500 for top-level jobs for which entering persons are qualified by previous experience.

Forestry: Foresters are actively concerned with the protection and conservation of one of our country's most vital resources: its forest lands. Fighting fire, insects, and disease, managing our lumber supplies to meet growing demands, protecting wildlife and water, providing expanding opportunities for outdoor recreation for our citizens—all these are part of the federally employed forester's duties.

To get such a job a bachelor's degree with major study in forestry or a closely related subject is required. There is a wide variety of stimulating work and broad choice as to place of employment. Most jobs are in the Department of Agriculture and offer alternating periods of outdoor and desk work. No written test is required.

Salaries: From about $4,600 to $5,540 to start.

Legal Work: All federal agencies employ some attorneys, and in numerous agencies a large proportion of the employees are lawyers (such as in the Department of Justice). There are about 8,000 attorney positions in all departments of our federal government.

To be a lawyer, one must first attend law school and pass the bar examinations of the state in which one resides. Then, when ready for your first "clerkship," consider the federal government as an employer. Attorney positions are not filled through regular Civil Service procedures: lawyers are hired directly by the agencies. Select the agency whose work interests you and apply directly. But remember, all employing agencies in this field require their *attorneys* to be members of the bar.

The word "attorneys" is emphasized because there are other government positions in the legal field that do *not* require admission to the bar, although they do require full professional legal training, i.e., a law degree. A large portion of the work of such legal assistants is in connection with claims filed with, by, or against the federal government. Some of these positions involve passing Civil Service written tests.

Attorneys prepare and argue cases, render legal advice and opinions, draft contracts, develop proposed legislation, and conduct investigations—a variety of legal work as diverse as that practiced outside the government.

Salaries: From about $4,600 to slightly over $14,500.

Medicine and Public Health: There are 11,000 civilian medical officers in the federal service. Almost three fourths of them work in hospitals and outpatient clinics of the Veterans' Administration, caring for and treating war veterans and doing medical research. They are hired on the basis of professional qualifications, training, and experience. All have their M.D. degrees. Salaries range from over $11,000 to about $17,000 a year.

Another 20 per cent of the medical officers in the federal service are members of the Commissioned Corps of the U.S. Public Health Service. They work in almost every aspect of medical and public health practice, from study of chronic diseases to the effects of radiation on the human body; from research to find a cure for the common cold to methods of increasing the life expectancy of our Indian and Alaskan native populations; from detection and prevention of communicable disease to efforts to stem the increasing danger from water and air pollution.

Entrance to the corps is by written examinations, and pay is the same as that given commissioned medical officers in our armed services. *Note:* Pension plans are particularly generous, both for the military and the USPHS.

The remaining 5 per cent of federally employed medical officers are in the regular Civil Service. They work side by side with the PHS officers and as civilians in the Army, Navy, and Air Force hospitals. They also adjudicate claims and do administrative work. Entrance salaries in 1963 ranged from $9,100 to $15,000.

BEFORE YOU ARE READY

A young person who is excited about any phase of career work in the federal government surely must have noted by now that almost every job described requires extensive education. This is especially true of professional jobs. But clerks and stenographers in government must also meet high standards. These nonprofessional jobs can be absorbing and rewarding; clerks and stenographers make the wheels of government go round!

It is wise to make the best possible grades in high school in both required and elective subjects in order to be eligible for the college of your choice. Once in college, consider carefully the kind of course that will lead to a public-service career in your special field of interest. This specialization need not rule out purely cultural pursuits such as art or the dance, though these are not likely to be of direct use in government work. (But they won't hurt you a bit in winning friends and widening your horizons in government.)

There are literally hundreds of positions in public service, not only at federal level, as described here, but in state, county, and municipal agencies. For information on these last three, write to your own state, county, or municipality. For more information on federal job opportunities, write as follows:

For federal positions in the specific occupation that appeals to you:

> U.S. Civil Service Commission
> Washington 25, D.C.

For Foreign Service positions:

> Board of Examiners for the Foreign Service
> Department of State
> Washington 25, D.C.

For commissioned medical officers' information:

> Division of Commissioned Officer Personnel
> U.S. Public Health Service
> Washington 25, D.C.

For medical officer positions in the Veterans' Adminstration:

> Veterans' hospital nearest you.

Winners of Rockefeller Public Service Awards

THE ORIGINAL PROGRAM

1952-53

BELL, DAVID E., Administrative Assistant to the President.

DURHAM, HOWARD E., Regional Director, Federal Mediation and Conciliation Service.

EVANS, W. DUANE, Chief, Division of Interindustry Economics, Bureau of Labor Statistics, Department of Labor.

HILBERT, GUIDO, Chief of Bureau of Agricultural and Industrial Chemistry, Department of Agriculture.

HOWARD, GEORGE W., Chief, Technical Service Department, Engineer Research and Development Laboratories, Department of the Army.

KIRKPATRICK, HELEN P., Public Affairs Adviser, Department of State.

SADY, EMIL, Chief, Pacific Division, Office of Territories, Department of the Interior.

SEIDMAN, OSCAR, Aeronautical Research Development and Design Engineer, Department of the Navy.

SHULMAN, MARSHALL D., Special Assistant to the Secretary of State, Department of State.

SIMON, DOROTHY M., Aeronautical Research Scientist, National Advisory Committee for Aeronautics.

YOUNG, MARTIN D., Head, Section of Epidemiology, National Institutes of Health, Department of Health, Education, and Welfare.

1953-54

ANFINSEN, CHRISTIAN B., Chemist, National Institutes of Health, Department of Health, Education, and Welfare.

BERGER, MARIE C., Office of the Legal Counsel, Foreign Operations Administration.

BOORMAN, HOWARD L., Vice Consul, Hong Kong, Department of State.

BRILL, DANIEL H., Economist, Board of Governors of Federal Reserve System.

BROWN, CLINTON E., Assistant Head, Gas Dynamics Branch, Langley Aeronautical Laboratory, National Advisory Committee for Aeronautics.

ISENBERGH, MAX, Deputy General Counsel, Atomic Energy Commission.

KELLEY, OMER J., Agricultural Administrator, Department of Agriculture.

KIDD, CHARLES V., Executive Secretary, Research Planning Council; Director, Research Planning Branch, National Institutes of Health, Department of Health, Education, and Welfare.

PORTER, ROBERT A., Chief, Operations Analysis Section, Air Proving Ground Command, Department of the Air Force.

RITZER, CHESTER F., Superintendent of Production, Ordnance Corps, Department of the Army.

WOOD, MARSHALL K., Technical Advisor to the Director, Comptroller Directorate of Management Analysis Service, Department of the Air Force.

1954-55

COLLIGAN, FRANCIS J., Executive Secretary, Board of Foreign Scholarships; Deputy Director, International Educational Exchange Service, Department of State.

DOUTY, HARRY M., Chief, Division of Wages and Industrial Relations, Bureau of Labor Statistics, Department of Labor.

ESGAIN, ALBERT J., Chief, International Law Branch, Office of the Judge Advocate General, Department of the Army.

HALL, SAMUEL R., Executive Secretary, Endocrinology Study Section, National Institutes of Health, Department of Health, Education, and Welfare.

KAUFMAN, FREDERICK, Chemist, Ordnance Corps, Department of the Army.

KOCH, ALBERT R., Chief, Banking Section, Board of Governors of Federal Reserve System.

NAMIAS, JEROME, Chief, Extended Forecast Section, Weather Bureau, Department of Commerce.

SANDERSON, FRED H., Chief, Regional Economic Staff, Office of Intelligence Research, Division of Research for Western Europe, Department of State.

SCHWARTZ, DAVID, Special Assistant to the Attorney General; Chief, Special Litigation Unit, Department of Justice.

SOUTHWORTH, HERMAN M., Research Assistant to Deputy Administrator for Marketing Research and Statistics, Department of Agriculture.

THOMAS, MARGARET E., Chief, Branch of Price Operations, Bureau of Labor Statistics, Department of Labor.

TREES, RICHARD (deceased), Physicist, National Bureau of Standards, Department of Commerce.

VINCENTI, WALTER G., Aeronautical Research Scientist, National Advisory Committee for Aeronautics.

1955-56

ANGELL, RICHARD S., Chief, Subject Cataloging Division; Acting Chief, Descriptive Cataloging Division, Library of Congress.

ARMSTRONG, WILLIS C., Deputy Director, Office of International Trade and Resources, Department of State.

CLOUD, PRESTON E., JR., Chief, Paleontology and Stratigraphy Branch, Geological Survey, Department of the Interior.

COHEN, MANUEL F., Counsel, Division of Corporation Finance, Securities and Exchange Commission.

FANO, UGO, Chief, Nuclear Physics Section, National Bureau of Standards, Department of Commerce.

GOLDSMITH, SELMA (deceased), Business Economist and Chief of Income Section, Department of Commerce.

HERSEY, ARTHUR B., Chief, Special Studies Section, Board of Governors of the Federal Reserve System.

HOUBOLT, JOHN C., Assistant Chief, Dynamic Loads Division, National Advisory Committee for Aeronautics.

JAEGERMAN, EDWARD C., Attorney-Adviser, Division of Trading and Exchanges, Securities and Exchange Commission.

MILES, RUFUS E., Comptroller, Department of Health, Education, and Welfare.

PEARCE, GEORGE W., Chief, Chemistry Section, Technical Development Laboratories, Department of Health, Education, and Welfare.

ROSENTHAL, ALBERT H., Regional Director, Department of Health, Education, and Welfare.

SHAPLEY, WILLIS H., Budget Examiner, Military Division, Bureau of the Budget.

SHISKIN, JULIUS, Chief Economic Statistician, Bureau of the Census, Department of Commerce.

VAN DERSAL, WILLIAM R., Assistant Administrator for Management, Soil Conservation Service, Department of Agriculture.

WEISS, RICHARD J., Physicist, Ordnance Materials Research Office, Department of the Army.

1956-57

BRANSCOMB, LEWIS M., Chief, Atomic Physics Section, National Bureau of Standards, Department of Commerce.

GREENE, LAWRENCE M., Assistant Director, Division of Corporate Regulation, Securities and Exchange Commission.

HORECKER, BERNARD L., Chief, Laboratory of Biochemistry and Metabolism, Department of Health, Education, and Welfare.

KATZ, SAMUEL I., Chief, British Commonwealth, Scandinavian and Near East Section, Federal Reserve Board.

MACDONALD, WENDELL D., Regional Director, Bureau of Labor Statistics, Department of Labor.

McCRENSKY, EDWARD, Director, Civilian Personnel and Services Division, Department of the Navy.

MORRELL, GERALD, Head, Rocket Combustion Section, Lewis Flight Propulsion Laboratory, National Advisory Committee for Aeronautics.

SEARLES, JOHN R., JR., Executive Director and Secretary, District of Columbia Redevelopment Land Agency.

SHURCLIFF, ALICE W., Labor Economist, Bureau of Labor Statistics, Department of Labor.

1957-58

EISENHART, CHURCHILL, Chief, Statistical Engineering Laboratory, National Bureau of Standards, Department of Commerce.

ENGLE, JAMES B., Italian Desk Officer, Bureau of European Affairs, Department of State.

JOHANNESSEN, KARL R., Meteorological Consultant to Hqs. Air Weather Service, Department of the Air Force.

JOHNSON, ROBERT H., Member of the Special Staff, National Security Council Staff.

LEBERGOTT, STANLEY, Analytical Statistician, Bureau of the Budget.

McNESBY, JAMES R., Physical Chemist, National Bureau of Standards, Department of Commerce.

MICKELSEN, WILLIAM R., Aeronautical Research Scientist, National Advisory Committee for Aeronautics.

ROSE, PAUL W., Director, USOM/Nepal, International Cooperation Administration.

UPSON, JOSEPH E., II, Research Geologist, Water Resources, Geological Survey, Department of the Interior.

1958-59

CHAPMAN, DEAN R., Aeronautical Research Scientist, National Aeronautics and Space Administration.

CHRIST, CHARLES L., Staff Associate, Geological Survey, Department of the Interior.

DAVID, LILY M., Chief, Branch of Current Wage Developments, Bureau of Labor Statistics, Department of Labor.

FANGET, LOUIS A., Chief, Publications Division, United States Information Agency.

FRANK, ISAIAH, Deputy Director, Office of International Trade, Department of State.

HELLER, HARRY, Assistant Director, Division of Corporation Finance, Securities and Exchange Commission.

MORTON, LOUIS, Deputy Chief, Histories Division, Office of Chief of Military History, Department of the Army (Resigned from Government Service and declined to use the award fellowship).

SCHAETZEL, J. ROBERT, Officer in Charge, Peaceful Uses of Atomic Energy, Department of State.

SCHNEIDERMAN, MARVIN S., Head, Section on the Therapeutic Trial, National Cancer Institute, Department of Health, Education, and Welfare.

SILVERMAN, ABNER D., Assistant Commissioner for Management, Public Housing Administration, Housing and Home Finance Agency.

STOVER, JAMES H., Head, Management Analysis Staff, Treasury Department.

THE REVISED PROGRAM

1960

BALL, ROBERT M., Deputy Director, Bureau of Old Age and Survivors Insurance, Social Security Administration, Department of Health, Education, and Welfare.

BOHLEN, CHARLES E., Special Assistant to the Secretary of State, Department of State.

HENDRICKS, STERLING B., Chief Scientist, Mineral Nutrition Laboratory for Pioneering Research, Department of Agriculture.

McARDLE, RICHARD E., Chief, Forest Service, Department of Agriculture.

NIEDERLEHNER, LEONARD, Deputy General Counsel, Department of Defense.

WIRTH, CONRAD L., Director, National Park Service, Department of the Interior.

1961

FELIX, ROBERT H., Director, National Institute of Mental Health, Department of Health, Education, and Welfare.

MERCHANT, LIVINGSTON T., U.S. Ambassador to Canada, Department of State.

NOLAN, THOMAS B., Director, Geological Survey, Department of the Interior.

STAATS, ELMER B., Deputy Director, Bureau of the Budget.

STAM, COLIN F., Chief of Staff, Joint Committee on Internal Revenue Taxation, U.S. Congress.

1962

BAUGHMAN, J. STANLEY, President, Federal National Mortgage Association, Federal Housing and Home Finance Agency.

CONLEY, REGINALD G., Assistant General Counsel, Department of Health, Education, and Welfare.

DRYDEN, HUGH L., Deputy Administrator, National Aeronautics and Space Administration.

HANSEN, MORRIS H., Assistant Director for Research and Development, Bureau of the Census, Department of Commerce.

THOMPSON, LLEWELLYN E., Ambassador to U.S.S.R., Department of State.

1963

ASTIN, ALLEN V., Director, National Bureau of Standards, Department of Commerce.

LOOMIS, HENRY, Director, International Broadcasting Service, U.S. Information Agency.

MARCY, CARL M., Chief of Staff, Foreign Relations Committee, U.S. Senate.

WEBER, EUGENE W., Chief, Civil Works Planning Division, Corps of Engineers, Department of the Army.

WESSENAUER, G. O., Manager of Power, Tennessee Valley Authority.